THE PRINCETON REVIEW

PRE-LAW
COMPANION

THE PRINCETON REVIEW

PRE-LAW COMPANION

The Ultimate Guide to Preparing for Law School

RON COLEMAN

Random House, Inc.
New York
http://www.randomhouse.com

Princeton Review Publishing, L.L.C.
2315 Broadway, 3rd Floor
New York, NY 10024

ISBN 0-679-77372-X

Edited by: Amy Zavatto
Designed by: Illeny Maaza

Manufactured in the United States of America on recycled paper

9 8 7 6 5 4 3

First Edition

Acknowledgments

This book is largely an outgrowth of the writing I have done over the last ten years for *Student Lawyer*, the magazine of the American Bar Association Law Student Division and where I have been a contributing editor from time to time. (Some of the material in this book originally appeared, in different form, in *Student Lawyer*.) In that connection thanks are due to former editors Lizanne Poppens and Sarah Hoban, who were too dumbfounded to ask why they needed an editorial intern. Credit goes to Jay Itzkowitz for pointing me in their direction.

Thanks are due as well to my clubmate and fellow after-dinner recreation aficionado Rob Case of The Princeton Review, for encouraging me to submit the proposal that became this book. In a different sense, lawyers Daniel H. Williams and Ronald Mysliwiec equally deserve thanks for unplugging me, each in his way, from my previous distractions.

The encouragement of my faithful parents, Terry and Jerry Coleman, my cousin, the writer Debra Kent, and friends such as Eli Wolf, Rabbi Menachem Zupnik, Gary Thompson, and Richard Szuch are gratefully acknowledged.

Yet the people due the most thanks in this regard are literary impresario Nick Viorst of Roundstone Press/Roundtable Press for his early and constant encouragement, and most of all my wife, attorney Jane Coleman. Her insight into law school and lawyering, her editorial acumen, and her support in the face of plainly inadequate recompense, have been invaluable. Thanks ultimately are due to "the *eybishter*," the One Above, for whatever I have and am, and Who is the true Opener of doors.

Contents

Preface

So you want to go to law school. Maybe.

You want advice about preparing for law school, how to decide where to go, how to apply. This book does that.

But to get to that part of the book, you must first "earn it." The first half of the *Prelaw Companion* is about who belongs in law school, what kinds of roles lawyers play, and what kind of work lawyers do.

This book isn't an obstacle course. It is about making sure you don't get caught up in the vortex of applying to law school without knowing why. Of course, you can skip right to chapter 6 if you've made up your mind. No alarms will go off.

If, however, there's a "maybe" out there—even a "definite maybe"— you will want to read the early chapters of the book, too. In fact, even if your definite is definite, why not apply the chicken soup test: "*It couldn't hurt.*" It couldn't hurt to be that much more aware of what law study will ask of you, and what you're getting yourself into and how you can best prepare for the experience.

Legal study attracts tens of thousands of the brightest, hardest-working, and most ambitious college students (and quite a few others) every year. Regardless of questions about whether it's a path you want to travel, you want to avoid the pitfalls, potholes, and pests. And you'd like a realistic picture of the landscape of the legal profession. The *Prelaw Companion*, therefore, functions as something of an introduction to the legal profession. By reading this book, you're already ahead of the game. You're willing to ask questions, and you're asking them at the right time.

Some people "end up" in law school because they don't know what else to do with themselves, especially after college graduation. They get there and discover that preparing for *admission* to law school is different from preparing for *success* in law school. And untold numbers aren't even at the right "there"; law school may be right for them, but they're at the wrong place at the wrong time.

Attending law school can transform your entire life. Despite the occasional joke (often only a mask for jealousy), most people still grant lawyers grudging respect, at least for their academic achievement. To others, a lawyer's station is exalted: She is a member of a learned profession, a gatekeeper at the levers of influence, an intercessor between the weak and the powerful. Lawyers are dominant in elective positions and throughout government; they wield power in business, media, and even entertainment.

Though less true than in the past, it is still the case that admission to the bar is a ticket to something of a club, a social caste. For many, the legal profession is a relatively fast, meritocratic entrée to upward mobility. And while there are tremendous variations within the profession, a legal career, in the scheme of things, can be lucrative. Lawyers are the highest-paid professionals, according to U.S. Census data analyzed in a 1995 *National Law Journal* article.

Yet the legal profession is changing, and fast. Many maintain that it is no longer a profession, dedicated to service, at all. Rather, they say, it is a business, one where "billable hours" are the product, attorneys the instruments of production, and clients are merely "inventory." In reality, both are true: the noble profession of the law must nevertheless recognize the business realities. Polls consistently reveal widespread unhappiness among lawyers with their work load, dissatisfaction with the typical substance of their labor, and pessimism about their future prospects. Entry into a top-line firm, once a ticket to a secure and comfortable professional future, now guarantees nothing but a high salary for an indefinite period, and the virtual death of non-professional life.

Still, the attraction of law school remains. Why?

Law school itself is expensive, time-consuming, and stressful. But it can also make you a better thinker, a better problem solver, a more knowledgeable player in business and civic life, and—most of all—*a lawyer*. For most people who go to law school, the experience defines not just their careers but a large part of their lives. It's a big decision. And well it should be, for the study of law will forever change the way you think and approach life's problems.

"Maybe," then, makes a lot of sense, for now. But you can't live at maybe forever. It won't pay the rent or make payments on your college loans. Certitude, however, isn't an end in itself. Law school only makes sense if it makes sense. And it has to make sense to you, for you, and you alone.

So you're going to be different. You're not going to be a prelaw zombie. If you follow through with your idea to attend law school, it will be because you have developed that idea into a strategy. After reading *The Prelaw Companion* you will have:

- inventoried your basic talents and skills and realistically concluded that you could *succeed* in law school and in the legal profession;

- established that you *want* to be a lawyer, at least in the medium run, and comprehended the reality of what kinds of economic opportunities lay ahead for new law school graduates;

- *planned* your undergraduate and other prelaw school experiences in a way consistent with your goal of attending law school;

- lined up whatever *resources* you need to make your plan a reality; and

- assessed—realistically—which law schools you're likely to get into, which of those you would want to attend, and your application strategy for maximizing your odds of *admission*.

In short, you will have made the most of this book.

CHAPTER ONE

A Look at Yourself

Now that you definitely, or maybe, or definitely maybe have decided on law school, how do you envision your future self? A dashing young professional? A soldier for social justice? Or perhaps a somewhat older version of yourself, in judicial robes?

If it's any of these, or even some variation on them, you've got the wrong idea dancing in your head—at least at this stage. Now is the time to look at yourself as you are today. You have to identify every wonderful feature you have and take a look at your imperfections and blemishes, too. It's a truism that law school (like anything else) is not for everybody. Now is the time to figure out if it's for you.

LAW SCHOOL IS FOR LAWYERS

Law schools are in the business of graduating people with the academic qualifications that, along with admission to a state bar, permit them to practice law. State bars require graduation from law school for anyone who wants to be admitted. It's a neat little package—law school is school for lawyers.

Almost any life experience, of course, can work to your benefit in a totally unrelated endeavor. Law school is no exception. Law school hones analytical ability and imparts a general familiarity with legal concepts. Would that come in handy if you wanted to become a writer? Probably. A fisherman? Maybe. A bond trader? Could be.

But that's beside the point. Military veterans often hearken back to their days in uniform as excellent preparation for all sorts of undertakings. Running a marathon is a great way to learn about dedication, commitment to a goal, and managing pain. Five years in prison might build character, too. But you're not about to do all of those things just because there are some incidental benefits to them.

Let's not beat around the bush: The only reason to consider attending law school is to become a lawyer.

THE BUSINESS TRACK

You will hear statements to the contrary. Some people would have you believe that law school is a good way to obtain a fancy, "doctorate" version of a business degree. "With an M.B.A., you're just an M.B.A., but with a J.D., you're a lawyer," says your Uncle Jay, chomping on a stogie as he dispenses another pearl of wisdom.

Uncle Jay's right, but his point just begs the question. A lawyer is a lawyer, not an M.B.A. If you want to go into business management, marketing, or finance, you won't learn how to do those things in law school. Nor will your post-graduation application for employment be received by corporations or investment banks as "better" than an application from a business school grad. They will see your resume and see a lawyer, and for good reason. You will have been trained for something, but not for business.

But isn't it true that a large percentage of top business executives are lawyers? Yes. *They're lawyers.* Get it? These are generally people who have performed at the top of the legal field, practicing law for anywhere from five to thirty years before making their way into the boardroom. Their experience in law and their practical experience in business (of course, they may *also* have M.B.A.s) qualifies them to run a company, a division, a studio, whatever. They will, however, have been lawyers first, and good ones.

Do as I Say, Not as I Did

Ron Friedman went straight from law school to management consulting at a top Boston consulting firm. It worked out great for him, but he doesn't recommend this path for everybody.

Friedman had worked as a financial forecaster for four years after college before enrolling at New York University School of Law. His summer work during law school convinced him that he didn't want to practice. Bypassing the NYU placement office, he sent out resumes to *business firms and landed a job as a consultant in strategic investing. It was, he says, solely on the strength of his previous experience that he got that job.*

Friedman is sure that he wasn't harmed by going to law school (except that it took him one more year to get his J.D. than it would have to get his M.B.A.) and says he has benefited from it. While many skills used in business, except perhaps the most sophisticated finance work, are learned on the job, he says that's not true for knowledge of the law. So why does he advise against others trying to do what he did?

Most law school graduates looking for non-legal work, says Friedman, come across as "damaged goods." Employers, he says, wonder about someone who spends three years at law school but doesn't want to be a lawyer. One way or another, that applicant has a lot to explain. The next resume on the stack, in contrast, simply won't raise questions.

Thus, Friedman reasons, the law school detour could be more harmful than helpful for most people who are ultimately interested in a business career. Despite his success, his advice is blunt: "People who go to law school should be sure they want to practice law."

THE POLITICS TRACK

It's true that if your name is Kennedy, you can go to law school and then be elected to national office before you even frame that license to practice. But for most people, law school makes little sense as a direct route into an elective or appointed office.

That doesn't mean it would hurt to be a law school graduate to get into politics. But put the expense, time commitment, and lost income of law school into the hopper, and the marginal benefit of attending law school usually doesn't add up. Most law school graduates who get into government (not counting government lawyers) have established themselves in law practice for many years and have become prominent through their professional accomplishments before they're asked to serve.

It's also true that one of Hillary Rodham's first jobs out of Yale law school was on Bernard Nussbaum's Watergate staff. And even graduates of other law schools are frequently welcome on legislative staffs to draft and analyze new laws. But this is lawyer work, not something else. Mrs. Clinton, after all, ultimately made her way to become a partner in an Arkansas law firm, not a member of Congress or governor or President. As for her husband, well, there are exceptions.

THE ACADEMIC TRACK

One of those exceptions is the one Bill Clinton took, which is to teach law (full-time) after graduation. Though some law schools actually prefer their faculty members to have practical experience before they start to teach law, many top academians proceed from law school graduation to prestigious judicial clerkship, straight onto a tenure-track position at a law school. Some never even take the bar exam.

If you see this track in your future, you obviously have a lot of self-confidence. It's open only to the very top graduates of top schools. (After graduating from the University of Arkansas, Clinton attended Oxford on a Rhodes scholarship, then enrolled at Yale Law School before landing his law-teaching job back in Little Rock.) The question, however, is whether teaching law is what interests you, as opposed to the general idea of being a professor.

If you have the right stuff for success in the competitive, publish-or-perish world of academia, you may do just as well or even better teaching a subject like history, economics, or political science. The advantage of taking this approach is that you may not have to pay a penny for your graduate education and may even get a fellowship that will help support you.

The disadvantage to satisfying your yen to teach in a non-legal field is that most law professors only have a law degree, the three-year J.D., or its predecessor, the LL.B. On the other hand, professorial jobs in most other disciplines require a Ph.D., a degree that usually takes more than twice as long to get as a J.D. does. Plus there's that small matter of the doctoral dissertation. (It's ironic, but most colleges require teachers to have a Ph.D. to teach high-school graduates but only an LL.B. or J.D. to teach law to college graduates.)

Law professors also get paid more, often much more, than those who teach non-professional subjects, even at the graduate level. This may not last. For a century or so there was an American Bar Association policy that mandated a certain salary level for law professors. Schools had to comply in order to receive and retain ABA accreditation, without which a law school may as well have been an all-night launderette as far as state bar admissions authorities were concerned. Under pressure from the Justice Department, however, the powerful bar organization has now dropped the policy. The ultimate results will be the opening of more, lower-paying, slots for law professors and a general decline in their salary level.

On the other hand, stars such as Laurence Tribe and Alan Dershowitz make extraordinary incomes practicing law or acting as consultants while on the Harvard faculty. While the leaders in almost any field can achieve this, it is true that many law professors are "of counsel" to, or otherwise affiliated with, some law practice. All of which brings us full circle. These people, after all, are practicing law.

ACTIVE PRACTICE

So while there are innumerable paths for personal satisfaction within the profession—a topic we'll examine more closely in chapter 2—the vast majority of "law-related" career ambitions can only be satisfied by practicing law. Do you want to practice law for some period of time, even if you don't want to spend a career as a lawyer? If the answer is no, don't write your name on the inside cover of this book, and check if you still have the receipt. You won't find any more encouragement here.

That isn't to say that law school only makes sense if you're willing to make a *lifetime* commitment to practicing. You can pay your dues as a lawyer and move on to something else, maybe something immensely satisfying. In fact, a few years of legal practice makes for a nice bridge to many subsequent choices. A long-term goal, far and away from law, is fine, as long as (1) it's not so far removed from the practice of law as to render attending law school irrelevant and (2) you're really prepared to practice law for several years as part of your investment in getting where you want to go.

There's a third criterion, too, because number (2) alone—a willingness to practice law—won't do it without one more thing: (3) the capacity to do it well.

THE RIGHT STUFF

It is, notwithstanding what Hollywood would have you believe, not sufficient to desire something for it to become possible. The author of this book had a fervent desire to be the toast of Broadway; alas, he is clumsy of foot and has a predilection for too much dessert, so it will never be.

If you want to practice law, chances are you can. But you should want to excel at what you do. You may be able to find a law school that will admit you and take your tuition money, but that doesn't mean you'll excel or succeed at law practice. If your goal is to find some non-law place to succeed, you're not likely to get there by means of mediocrity as a lawyer, though with the help of Providence you may get there despite it.

What, then, is the right stuff? What are the basic ingredients of success at being a lawyer?

THE AVERAGES OF LAW

If you are an "average" person, you almost certainly will be a below-average lawyer. Remember, most law schools admit students with impressive academic credentials. It doesn't mean you'll be any less of a person, just less of a lawyer. Successful lawyers are above average. By average, of course, I am not referring to your height, weight, or girth. Rather, you have to be above average in at least one of two things: talent or ambition.

TALENT

Talent is, strictly speaking, a natural endowment, but that of course is only a beginning. The great tenor Luciano Pavarotti has a God-given talent that most experts agree is of historic proportion. But for all anyone knows, his uncle Luigi, the mandolin salesman, would have been even better. For whatever reason, Luigi didn't develop his gift. Talent must be nurtured and developed. Pavarotti has spent his life learning his craft, honing his talent. Thus, any definition of the word implies not just aptitude, but ability.

Some talents, such as Pavarotti's, generally don't lend themselves to application in the legal profession. They may even be antidotes to success, because a frustrated artist will never be appreciated in any adequate measure in the legal profession. Generally speaking, the greater the talent, the greater the frustration, and a legal career—with its great psychic and practical demands—will only become a source of resentment.

So, what are the applicable talents that are tapped in the field of law? Two of the more prominent are intelligence and expression.

Intelligence

A lot of things are easy for smart people. This insight may seem less than novel to some readers, but this is an exercise in evaluation. Getting into law school is less difficult today than it's been in many years, but getting into law school is no guarantee that the mental firepower is there for professional success and satisfaction.

Every lawyer needs the ability to think analytically, to focus on the important things, and ignore irrelevant distractions. To use a very simple example:

Judges and lawyers understand that illegally-obtained evidence cannot be admitted in a criminal trial. The heinousness of the crime or the defendant's long police record may be of great interest to the press and the fellows in the barber shop. But in legal thinking, these are irrelevant to the question of whether the evidence can be introduced.

Even direct evidence of the defendant's involvement in the crime— a videotape of his committing the act—would not affect the admissibility of *this* evidence. These are distractions. If the police found the murder weapon in an illegal search of the suspect's apartment, the murder weapon would not be considered evidence, no matter what other collateral information tried to affect that decision.

The fact that all good lawyers have analytical ability (which law school hones) explains why non-lawyers think attorneys are "playing lawyer games" during a heated discussion as well as in a court proceeding. It isn't a game. It's the application of rigid logic and a focus on the issue at hand. That kind of analysis is frustrating to those who can't follow it.

Do you have a talent for analysis? Consider your experiences with algebra, geometry, or calculus. (We will discuss the "prelaw" curriculum in chapter 6.) People with science and math backgrounds usually "get a pass" on this one. Having done well in math is not the point, however. The question is: Did you find it impossibly frustrating as opposed to just boring?

A slightly different way of conceptualizing this ability is describing a person as "problem oriented." Lawyers spend all day solving problems. Ironically, clients are fond of saying that "lawyers are deal-breakers, not deal-makers." Clients are disappointed when lawyers "break the deal" by informing them, for example, that their proposed approach to structuring that leveraged buyout is indeed brilliant but is also illegal in all fifty states. In reality, clients bring lawyers problems. The lawyer earns her pay by solving them and by identifying and solving other problems that the client didn't even know he had.

The ultimate question is whether you enjoy, and are good at, separating a complicated thing into component parts in order to understand it. That is the dictionary definition of analysis, the lawyer's stock-in-trade.

Analytical ability also implies the ability to improvise, to blaze a new trail toward the solution to a problem. For example, it's not too hard to learn the rules for routinely filing a publicly-held corporation's annual report. But what if the rules don't address a radical change in circumstances? How do you apply the rules when the chairman of the board and a bloc of shareholders are engaged in a court fight that brings all corporate activity to a halt? Or when the corporation declares bankruptcy? How about when the accountant who certified the report has just been busted for fraud?

Another reason lawyers must have good intellectual ability is that they simply have to learn a lot of material. For one thing, just getting through law school and the bar exam require assimilation of a lot of information. While rote memorization is not a big issue in actual practice, lawyers must *know* things, such as the principles of law and procedures that apply in their fields. Whether you can memorize the names of cases is not the point. What matters is that you can learn and internalize the legal concepts for which the cases stand.

Finally, many of the ideas and concepts that a lawyer must master are complex, to say the least. They're abstract, often requiring the mastery of a specific model or paradigm in addition to the ability to apply real or hypothetical facts to the model. Some problems lawyers face combine quantitative and non-quantitative factors in tandem, such as in analyzing the tax consequences of a transaction, planning an estate, or working out a deferred cash settlement for a personal-injury client.

You have to be honest about your analytical talent, both in terms of raw ability and how much you enjoy employing that ability. There are places in the legal profession for those with less analytical skill, but they may not be places you want to be.

Expression

Imagine a state-of-the art computer with a lightning-fast central processor, a river of RAM, enough hard-drive space to store the serial numbers of every dollar in Bill Gate's mattress—but no monitor. Such a computer would be great for storing and processing information, but if a human being wanted to sit down and make use of this wealth of knowledge, speed, and accuracy, the computer would be virtually useless.

Get the subtle analogy? You can have the keenest legal mind of all your peers, but if you can't translate what's in that noggin of yours, it's of no help to your clients, your employer, or yourself. Law is perhaps the most verbal of professions. A lawyer must have the ability to express himself clearly and convincingly. All the mental acumen in the world won't do a lawyer's clients or colleagues any good if he can't get his thoughts across. (Judges in particular are not prone to mind-reading.) The lawyer must not only vividly convey the analytical process that has gotten her to the conclusion, she must also express it in a way so that even the client will understand.

The issue here is verbal expression, which does not necessarily mean oral expression. Not everyone in the legal profession is expected to be Clarence Darrow, much less Cicero. In fact, less and less lawyering is done standing up in front of groups and talking. In litigation, clients don't want to spend the money, and judges don't have the time, for every motion (an application or request to the court) to include formal oral argument. In transactional or corporate law, electronic mail, teleconferencing, and video conferencing—plus the expense of travel and accommodations—are making the big, formal meeting, complete with canned presentations, something of a dinosaur.

All this, however, only enhances the importance of written communication. Every single lawyer, even a commodity-law expert whose entire practice boils down to a mastery of the regulations in the market for chinchilla futures, is at least in part an advocate. Every lawyer reports to a colleague or client who needs to know what the lawyer has figured out for that $150, $250, or $350 an hour. Whether it's in a written memorandum for internal or client use, a brief to the court, or the most common and arguably most important form of attorney writing—correspondence—to succeed, a lawyer must be a master of expression.

Legal Literates

Good writing skills will vault you to the top in law school. Besides leading to a good legal writing grade (in schools where it's graded), your substantive grades will reflect your ability to write exams.

Students of the humanities should not, however, think that this is where they get one over on the engineers and other digitheads. The fact is that the orderly, methodical training of scientists is an excellent foundation for good legal writing.

Writing style is important, but it's secondary to sense. Thus, most people with engineering and similar backgrounds do well in legal writing. You can't really fudge equations and circuits; they go or they don't. Conversely, some talented and expressive creative writers have a hard time adapting to the rigors of legal writing. They usually need to make some spiritual adjustments. Their natural affinity for the written word, however, will eventually stand them in good stead.

If you haven't had much practice in writing, there's no need to panic. Almost everyone can learn the fundamentals, though for some people they come much harder than for others.

Probably the main thing to worry about is if you're the kind of person who, if asked to name a book she read in the last year, couldn't think of one. Every good writer is an avid reader. Turn off the tube and crack a book. You must be comfortable with the enterprise of written expression if you want to be a lawyer. Lawyers live in a world of words. Ultimately, those who can develop and convey an idea in a compelling writing style will write their own tickets.

AMBITION

Having said all that, there are times when a surfeit of talent can be overcome with drive and ambition. There are many happy, successful lawyers with limited talent but lots of ambition and focus. Indeed, there are plenty of profoundly talented but unmotivated lawyers who are miserable.

Much of law practice is attention to detail, repetition, and effort. Some smart guys aren't so good at these things; they like things that come easy. Every day, in courtrooms across the fruited plain, one of these prodigies gets his head handed to him by a seemingly innocuous adversary who's done her homework, sweated the details, and cares about her client.

Hard-working, ambitious, and personable people who may not have the most stellar resumes will often have flourishing practices. Any area where dealing with people is as least as important as dealing with statutes is an area where someone who's willing to apply himself can succeed.

None of this is to say that there are too many successful lawyers who are, shall we say, intellectually challenged. There are hardly any, besides the phonies who will probably always manage to attach themselves to the gravy train one way or another. Everyone who wants to practice law has to have at least common sense and a good dose of analytical ability. But with a little talent, effort and conscientiousness can go a long way.

And the ones who have super brains *and* super hustle? They're the best. But what if you don't fit into the latter category and lack that one-two punch? Don't despair. There's still room for the rest of us average Joes and Josephines.

CHAPTER TWO

The Lawyer Personality

LAWYER, KNOW THYSELF

The person interested in a legal career doesn't have to be outgoing, aggressive, or argumentative to succeed as a lawyer. There is a limit to how high a wallflower can grow, especially in certain fields. But the more talent on hand, the less you have to worry about personality.

In this regard, the legal profession is like any other. Walk up and down the aisle at a law firm or attend the bar association dinner, and you'll meet personalities there as diverse as any other gathering.

On the other hand, extremes are never good. Someone who simply cannot emerge from his shell has no business in the courtroom. If your desire is to be the next Perry Mason, it's best not to be someone who gets cold sweats at the prospect of making eye contact with his pharmacist or to have a voice that can only be heard by dogs. On the other hand, a bombastic, life-of-the-party type is unlikely to enjoy the largely cerebral pleasures of patent law.

There are exceptions, of course. For example, one of the most prominent trusts and estates lawyers in a major northeastern state—let's call him Tank—has a personality that makes George Steinbrenner look like Bob Newhart. He bellows at secretaries, lambastes associates, and, by all indications, kicks puppies while wearing cleats. But with his clients—many of them frail and elderly—Tank is the model of deference and charm. He has done very well for himself. Clients love him.

Ultimately, you can rest assured that there are few personalities that can't be accommodated within the legal profession. However, there are certain personality traits that you must have to succeed in law.

The necessity of being a "people person" is clear when you comprehend the importance of collaboration in legal work. Whether a solo practitioner or part of a firm with hundreds of lawyers and offices all over the world, you must be able to work with others (whether or not you make friends with them). Every lawyer must collaborate with her colleagues, support and paralegal staff, clients, judges, and adversaries. Co-authoring an appellate brief, working out a complex litigation strategy, putting together a "mega-deal," or hammering out a settlement all require an ability to work effectively with people. Which brings us to the magic bullet of success: attitude.

ATTITUDE

Some personality traits are not only important to the legal profession, but also fundamental to the way you go through life. These traits are known collectively as "attitude."

Sometimes "attitude" is a code word for "willingness to submit." Like anything else, this depends on whose hands you're in. Figuring out whether or not the proper attitude is something you possess may be the most important element of deciding if a career in law is right for you.

So what makes up attitude? There are numerous ways to divide it up. We think there are three main elements. If you're missing any one of these, you may last in the legal profession, but not very long—no matter what size your brain. They are:

- A good work ethic

- Perseverance

- Humility

You don't need this book to define these terms. But we can consider how they apply to being a lawyer, particularly during the early years of an attorney's career.

A GOOD WORK ETHIC

Law school is a lot of work. You have whole new subjects to master, subjects that require, to different degrees, a whole new way of thinking. After graduation, the bar exam makes law school look like spring break. Then the worst is over, right? Well, not exactly.

You'll never do anything like the bar exam again (unless you fail it), but as a lawyer, you're in the real world of work. Most lawyers work hard. That's why you'll hear people say, "the law is a jealous mistress." There are two main reasons a legal career is so time-consuming: market forces and the natures of lawyers and the law business (under virtually any market conditions) themselves.

Many attorneys are paid quite well, enormously well, to work so hard, while others whose labor is no lighter make peanuts. Where do all these people fit in the employed-attorney stratum? Let's take a look.

Supply and Demand

At the bottom of the earnings scale, public interest lawyers, public defenders, and city prosecutors juggle hundreds of cases, too swamped to give virtually any of them the time they really deserve. The demand for their services has burgeoned while the money to pay them has withered.

Many small firms and sole practitioners dare not refuse any business that comes their way, no matter how busy they are at the moment. They live in terror of the boom-and-bust cycle that may leave them idle in a legal services sellers' market. Others are better established and have a steady flow of business; some positively print money, and are able to sell personal attention, low overhead, and of course, high quality. The possibilities in small firms are much like that in any other small business.

In large law firms in the biggest cities, associates are expected to put in enough time to bill their firms' clients at least 2,000 hours a year, but they frequently work 2,400, 2,600, or more. In cities and other populated areas, salaries are set by a local standard that is usually irrelevant to the financial realities in a given law firm. In order to compete for desirable candidates, many firms set starting salaries higher than makes sense in their own economic scheme. To finance those salaries, the firms look for increased productivity from associates (junior lawyers who are employees of the firm's partners). "Productivity" is what bosses call lots of work.

Quest for Fire

Meanwhile, up the food chain, partners are working harder than ever. They do it to satisfy their egos, meet their mortgages, or just to pay associate and support salaries and rent at a fancy address. No matter how successful, many lawyers find it hard to turn down work—even if it doesn't necessarily look as if it will pay.

Lawyers are by nature ambitious people, as we've established already, and every new case is fuel to the fires in their bellies. It's a chance to prove themselves, stretch themselves, and maybe make another buck or two.

Alan Lowenstein is founder of Lowenstein, Sandler, Kohl, Fisher & Boylan, one of New Jersey's most respected (and profitable) law firms. He graduated from the Harvard Law School in 1936 and never looked back. Though now officially retired from management of the 145-lawyer firm, he still trudges in with new clients and fresh enthusiasm for his work. He certainly doesn't have to do it anymore. So why is it that lawyers work so hard?

"I guess the successful lawyer keeps attracting more and more business," he says. "Since even when you practice in partnership you still feel as if you're on your own . . . lawyers are a little bit afraid to turn down a client. The new case could be interesting. And you don't know if there's going to be another one.

"In former days there was a professional pride in doing things of interest and in doing things of service to the community, by which you incidentally made money," continues Lowenstein, once known as "Mr. Newark" for his tireless civic devotion to the city. "But I think the professional curiosity of taking on a new and exciting case was something that made it hard to turn down."

There is a certain pride lawyers take in giving themselves over to their careers. Sometimes, though, it becomes an unstoppable, indefatigable cycle, as partners begin to look askance at those of their number (much less associates) who "aren't pulling their weight." If your idea of working late includes the phrase, "Can I go now?" you haven't gotten it yet. Take off your watch and put it in your top drawer, next to the highlighters. Everyone will go home when the job is done. If you're not afraid of the great oxymoron, "a little hard work," you'll be in good shape in law school and beyond.

Hard But Bite-Sized

FWAs (Flexible Work Arrangements) are a lot like New Year's Resolutions. Everyone makes them but no one ever does anything about them. A report by the Committee on Women in the Legal Profession of the Association of the Bar of the City of New York concludes, however, that there's a lot more the profession could do about FWAs, and that everyone would be better off if it did.

The report, published in the June 1995 edition of The Record, decries the relegation of non-traditional work schedules to the category of "part-time work," with its implication of less-than-full commitment. Primarily authored by Jolie Schwab, an attorney at Capital Cities/ABC in New York, the report quotes a 1994 report by the National Association for Law Placement that says 86 percent of law offices nationwide claim to offer part-time scheduling, but only 2 percent of all attorneys actually work such schedules.

Schwab herself worked three days a week in her five years at a law firm because she had a child at home but eventually was forced to leave as her firm phased out part-timers. Now she works on a job-share basis at Capital Cities. "We overlap a day a week, and talk from home." The advantage of the job share, she says, is that "you really don't have to worry about it, because on the days you're not there someone's covering for you."

Most lawyers interested in FWAs are men and women seeking to have some part in raising their children while participating in a highly competitive career in a society where working parents are the norm. Others, however, need time to care for aged parents, "or serve their communities in other ways," says the report.

Part-time isn't the only kind of FWA, although most have much to prove for application to the legal profession. The report says that some lawyers are able to carry a full load in compressed workweeks. Others share jobs, telecommute, or work flextime.

Employers benefit from FWAs, the report says, because they can boost productivity and morale, help retain employees, enhance professional growth by the development of "well-rounded" lawyers, give the employer concomitant flexibility in scheduling, enhance a firm's "progressive" image, and reduce fixed costs. The report says that, notwithstanding these prospective advan-

tages, a body of myths about FWAs—including effects on profitability, professional commitment, client relations, matter management, and the "opening the floodgates" effect—prevent their more widespread use.

The report recognizes the obstacles to FWAs in a profession where the main commodity being sold is lawyers' time. "A great deal of downsizing has taken place in the legal profession," the article continues. "Fewer people are expected to do ever increasing volumes of work for less money. However, somehow these trends must be reconciled with the increasing pressures on the American family. Encouraging FWAs may be one way to do this."

PERSEVERANCE

It sounds like "hard work," and sometimes it leads to hard work, but it's a little different. Perseverance is doggedness, stubbornness, a refusal to take no for an answer when you need a "yes." No one ever compared lawyers to moms, but, like a mother, a lawyer's work is never done. And this, too, is an important source of professional pride.

It's a thoroughness thing. If a lawyer is doing legal research, how can he ever know he's unearthed every possible case that could bear on the question? If he's fleshing out the facts in a heated litigation, how many stones must he look under until he can say none have been left unturned? A lawyer checking a document, such as a major filing with federal securities regulators, never really knows if he's missed a mistake that could upend the entire filing—weeks or months of work and the financial future of a corporate client down the drain. You can never prove a negative, so how does a lawyer know there's no more work to do?

He doesn't. He just has to follow the trail until it goes cold and hope for the best. The budget for the project could have an impact on that calculus. But there's not a lawyer worth his salt who hasn't gone past a budgeted number of hours to log onto the online legal research service from her home computer, using her own time to check that one new angle she thought of on the way home.

If you're a "four-fifths" kind of person—someone who's great on the first 80 percent of a job but not a closer—it could be rough sledding in the legal profession. Thoroughness can't be faked. Woe to the associate who leaves that last fifth for someone senior to him, much less a partner, to complete. He'll never see the last fifth of his career.

Are you someone who's motivated to get the job done right, no matter how long it takes? It may require sacrifices of other interests, some near and dear, but for such a person, thoroughness is as a matter of personal honor. You may have demonstrated it on your junior paper, at rehearsals for the musical revue, or looking after someone else who needed your care. If you can honestly assess yourself in this way, you possess a quality that will serve you well in the legal profession, as well as anywhere else.

HUMILITY

What, of all things, does humility have to do with being a lawyer?

It doesn't mean, in trial-law terms, admitting to your adversary or the court that your client's position is weak, or that you're really pushing too hard on her behalf, or that the evidentiary objection you made wasn't really very valid. Though there may be times for strategic retreats, your client, whether in court, at the conference table, or in dueling correspondence, is entitled to a bold, confident advocate.

You will never, however, get into a courtroom, or a conference room, or even send out your own correspondence unless you learn Shaolin-priest-style humility. As a young associate, your "masters"—senior associates and partners—may not be the ethical or spiritual giants you may expect to meet in a Buddhist monastery, but they know a lot more law than you do, law review or not. And they knew enough to have hired you.

You must be someone who can learn from his superiors and from his mistakes, someone who can take criticism like a mensch. This means:

- admitting the mistakes were mistakes

- virtually never offering excuses

- seeking to understand what you did wrong

- seeking to understand why you did it wrong

- never making the same mistake twice

There is a caveat in this learning-from-your-mistakes scenario. The law game is now played, especially in larger firms, for very high stakes. The deals are big, the litigations are big, the money is big. There is less and less tolerance for the mistakes of junior people. In these mammoth organizations, it can be years before you even get to look at the ball, much less run with it.

What does that have to do with humility? When you do get your chance, you must diligently figure out as much as possible in advance, ask for advice from those more experienced, and admit when you're in over your head. This requires an even greater application of humility than the post-mortem kind.

And what of the brave soul who graduates law school, perhaps with a few clinical courses and some summer experience under her belt, hangs out a shingle and just starts practicing? Where's the humility in that? Talk to someone who's succeeded that way. Chances are you'll find one of the most humble people you ever met.

THE CHARACTER ISSUE

One more thing. Notwithstanding what you may have heard, you should not consider law school if you're a crook, a swindler, a fake, a phony, or a fraud.

Truth, Justice, and the American Way

This section is not about being motivated in your career by a desire for justice or truth. If that motivation can propel you through the realities of practice you are among the lucky few. The desires for social justice, constitutional reform, or better government are valuable in any member of society, and in a lawyer they can be great attributes as lawyers are specially poised to effect these changes in society. But these desires can also, if not tempered by realism, make law practice more painful than pleasurable.

However, these qualities are not the topic for this chapter, because most lawyers simply don't deal with these issues on a daily basis, if at all. Most lawyers' jobs are to help people or businesses with money protect it or increase it. You may or may not agree that this is a morally neutral activity. But there it is.

Idealism is simply not a *prerequisite* for law practice. Lawyers provide a service. The parties or causes to whom you hitch your wagon may make all the difference in the world to you, but the focus of this chapter is whether your wagon is street legal in the first place.

The Attorney in the Three-Piece Toga

Is cynicism a valuable trait for a lawyer?

Before you answer, ask yourself if you know the meaning of the word. It comes from Greek. A Cynic was a member of a school of Greek philosophy who believed that the only good was virtue, and that the essence of virtue lay in self control and independence.

A cynic (with lower case "c"), on the other hand, is defined as "a fault-finding, capricious critic, especially someone who believes that human conduct is motivated wholly by self interest." Oscar Wilde said it was someone who knew the price of everything and the value of nothing.

It is possible for the vaunted "critical thinking" and analysis of law school to go haywire and become cynicism. Law students are taught early on that their heads are "full of mush," and they must learn to undermine assumptions and identify unstated premises. By the time they come home for Thanksgiving, some first-years have become so adept at probing and questioning that when the time comes to carve the turkey, even the dog won't sit next to them. "Legal thinking" is such a seductive and powerful analytical tool that it can make you forget that it is of little value in matters involving human character and emotion, much less faith.

"Skepticism is essential for a lawyer," says David Montgomery, a partner of the New York construction-litigation firm of Sacks Montgomery. "Professionally, you can't accept things on faith," he adds. "But there are some things in life, especially in personal relations, you do need to accept on faith."

Montgomery explains that law schools are rife, not with cynics, but with idealists. As students leave the ivory tower, they learn that judges are more, and less, than the finely-honed opinions taught in law school. "You come to realize that they're human beings who put their robes on one arm at a time," he says. That lesson, however, is a loss of illusion, not idealism. Mature skepticism is a manifestation of self control and independence of mind. This separation of reality from illusion can actually be the foundation of an adult idealism—which is to say, a philosophy of virtue. Perhaps a lawyer should be a Cynic, after all.

PRACTICAL ETHICS

On a practical basis, lawyers have tremendous ethical responsibilities, both to their clients and to society (usually, in that order). There are times (such as when a lawyer knows that her client is a threat to life or, in some states, property) when he is obligated to go so far as to alert the authorities of the danger. Attorneys are frequently guardians of other people's lives and property. The law invests them with presumptions of honesty and good faith. People who run afoul of the law may, in some circumstances, be punished less severely because they can show that they "acted on the advice of counsel."

But lawyers are regulated severely. Most serious lapses of ethical behavior are eventually discovered, and their perpetrators severely punished. One slip-up can endanger, or even end, decades of professional life. Consider a sampling of one month's worth of attorney disciplinary dispositions by New Jersey State Supreme Court. Many of the offenses will seem familiar to fans of television and movies. The distinction is that in real life, actions have consequences (and that in real life, the names aren't changed to protect the guilty):

CASE	OFFENSE	DISPOSITION
In the Matter of Sidney K. (attorney admitted in 1972)	Failure to cooperate in a pending ethics investigation	Suspended from the practice of law until further order of the court
In the Matter of Henry W. (attorney admitted in 1963)	Misusing funds erroneously credited to his trust account by his bank	Disbarred for life
In the Matter of Frank F. (attorney admitted in 1986)	Gross neglect in required recordkeeping, failure to act with reasonable diligence, failure to communicate with a client, failure to turn funds over promptly to the person to whom they are due, failure to cooperate with disciplinary authorities	Disbarred for life
In the Matter of Joseph J. (attorney admitted in 1985)	Misappropriation of client funds	Disbarred for life
In the Matter of Carlos F. (attorney admitted in 1988)	Failure to pay a fee arbitration award to a former client	Suspended from the practice of law until further order of the court, and a sanction of $500
In the Matter of *William B.* (attorney admitted in 1967)	Failure to inform his clients of information he had about other parties' interest in a transaction involving his client	Suspended from the practice of law for three months
In the Matter of David B. (attorney admitted in 1959)	Arranging sham marriages for the purpose of misleading the Immigration and Naturalization Service	Suspended from practice pending final resolution of ethics proceedings
In the Matter of Michael M. (attorney admitted in 1984)	Theft of mail	Suspended from practice for three years
In the Matter of Richard W. (attorney admitted in 1973)	Failure to cooperate in an ethics investigation	Suspended from practice until further notice

Heaven forbid that anyone looking in a mirror sees any of these guys staring back.

There are, of course, ethical transgressions that are harder to catch, or are less obvious than the ones cited above. You don't have to be ready to pocket other people's money to commit a violation of legal ethics. And ethical lapses aren't only the lot of desperate hustlers and strung-out alcoholics. Lawyers constantly face the temptations for unethical behavior. Here are a few examples:

- A litigation attorney is asked to draft pleadings or other papers that close that little gap in the case, say, the part about the client having a pre-existing medical condition, with a little white lie.

- A smoking-gun document is uncovered in an investigation—does the lawyer produce it to the other side when she's confident (well, 99 percent anyway) that, once it goes into the shredder, it will never be heard of again?

- A transactional lawyer is asked to draft papers that amount to nothing more than an illegal tax dodge.

- An environmental lawyer is asked to convey his client's promise that a deadly poison will no longer be produced at the client's factory, even though the lawyer knows it will be weeks before operations are shut down.

Advocacy can slip into untruthfulness so smoothly that you don't notice. Pressure to do the not-quite-right thing can come from a supervising partner, a panicked client, or your own credit card statements.

Personal Ethics

Finally, beyond actual unethical behavior, you have to ask yourself how far your personal ethics will take you within the bounds of legal ethics. The best criminal lawyers, after all, are the ones who usually get *guilty* people out of trouble. Could you defend a wealthy socialite who murders his ill wife with a hypodermic needle? The killer of a minority group member whose victim identifies him with his dying breath? A jealous ex-husband who knifes his former wife and her companion to death?

Criminal law is the most obvious source of these conflicts, but they exist in many areas of practice. Lawyers just doing their jobs are not always doing the right thing for society; sometimes, they are helping their clients do something awful. You need to decide if you can do this job and still look in the mirror.

CHAPTER THREE

It's a Lawyer's Life

You've gone through chapters 1 and 2 and determined that you have the basic equipment necessary to succeed at law school and, no less important, in the legal profession. Now the question is whether you want to apply your talent, ambition, personality, and ethical sense to a career in the law.

To answer that, you need to make two inquiries: Whether you *can* do the kinds of things lawyers do, and whether you are *interested* in the work lawyers do.

This chapter is about the kinds of things that lawyers do, discussed in terms of the roles they play almost every day. (The work lawyers do will be discussed in chapter 4.) You can use this discussion to continue the self-assessment process begun in the last chapter. It will also give you a head start on chapter 7, on how to prepare for law school.

As you go through this chapter, monitor your gut reaction to the types of activities and skills discussed. They're fairly universal; most lawyers do these kinds of things and apply these kinds of skills, regardless of their specialties. If indeed you're on the right track in thinking about law school, most of them should excite you, intrigue you, or at least challenge you in a positive way.

WHAT ALL LAWYERS DO

Whether drafting a will, defending someone accused of a crime, or delving into the mysteries of environmental regulation, all lawyers play a number of roles in achieving their goals—that is, serving their clients' legal needs as well as developing professionally.

Paul Brest, Dean of Stanford Law School, recently outlined a cross-disciplinary approach to teaching law, which his school is developing. He identified certain roles that lawyers must master to succeed. Given Stanford's leading role in legal education, we'd like to adapt Dean Brest's analysis to our discussion.

The basic roles of a lawyer are as follows. (Note that some of these "jobs" are actually subsets of other ones, as demonstrated in the discussion below.)

- Analyst and researcher of legal rules

- Investigator

- Counselor

- Problem solver, decision maker, and planner

- Advocate and negotiator

- Architect of transactions and organizations

ANALYZING LEGAL RULES: THE CASE METHOD

The case method is the classical training for "thinking like a lawyer." Its purpose is the mastery of doctrine (legal rules) and analysis (here, application of those rules to a factual situation). The basics of the case method are supposedly a variation on the deductive method employed by Socrates in his philosophical discourses (hence the phrase "Socratic method"). Indeed, many students still insist that the method is Greek to them.

Under the case method, you read "cases," reported or published appellate court decisions collected in a "casebook." These introduce you to principles of law in the process of applying them to a fact situation. In class, the professor (if he is teaching in the classical mode) interrogates a member of the group on the rationale behind the rule, what differences in the fact pattern would make her change her mind, how far she would extend the rule. Some people find this terrifying; others, exhilarating. Either way, it's an experience seldom experienced again after law school, save in arguing before an appeals court or going on job interviews.

Examinations are based on "issue-spotting." You're given a complex factual situation and are asked to identify the "legal issues," usually described as the respective parties' rights and responsibilities. In many circumstances, this is what lawyers do when clients, partners, or supervisors contact them and tell them they have new matters for them to handle.

In the case method learning process, the student ideally internalizes the system by which legal rules are developed, learned, and applied. Thus, the skills of legal analysis, a skepticism of superficial reasoning, and, to some extent, the beginnings of professional judgment all begin to be developed within the student.

The most successful legal analysts succeed in actually convincing a judge to *change* doctrine. They do this by broadening their analysis to hearken to a larger doctrine than the one supposedly at issue, such as a broad legislative scheme, a trend in court decisions, or a constitutional fiat.

RESEARCH IN LAW

Most real-life situations are more complicated than the kind you read about in law school, however. The editors of legal texts usually want to make one point at a time, so they edit out the "irrelevant" details. As you get more advanced in your practice, you're exposed to more and more of those details. This is when you apply your issue spotting skills, based on the doctrine (legal rules) you've already learned.

Though you'll learn lots of rules in law school (and probably even more while studying for the bar exam), the learning never stops. You learn more in active practice through legal research, the mechanics of which are taught during the first year of law school. Legal research applies the analytical skills you learned in law school and builds on the basic doctrines in the areas of law you've studied—such as the law of contracts, of torts (non-contractual, non-criminal injuries), or of property. Then you apply what you've learned to a specific situation.

As your research continues, you may go back to the fact pattern and take a closer look at facts that you first thought irrelevant. That's because you may find legal precedents in cases whose rules turn on facts you'd previously filtered out. Indeed, based on your research, you may find that more factual investigation is necessary (see below).

JUST THE FACTS, MA'AM

For the century following the introduction of the case method into legal study by Harvard's Christopher Columbus Langdell, legal analysis was supposed to be the whole of skills that a lawyer needed. It is a technique well suited to dealing with situations where the facts are already set. Thus, it is useful in litigation about an event or transaction that already took place, and particularly in appeals, where the facts of a case are no longer open to dispute.

Of course, in most situations faced by lawyers, the relevant facts either are in dispute (often heated) or are prospective. In the former case, the attorney must investigate the facts and try to "develop" a fact pattern that, based on the doctrine the lawyer knows or has learned in his research, is most helpful to his client's legal position. In this case, the lawyer falls back on his legal analytical skills. Why? Because factual investigation is not taught through the case method or hardly even hinted at. Yet the premise of the case method is full knowledge of the facts.

All but the most cynical lawyer will agree that, all things being equal (no, they hardly ever are equal, but still), it is the *facts* that win the case. That is: Did he really hit that guard rail? Was the light really green? How fast was the driver of the other car going? Having the right facts is what makes a "good case"; having the wrong facts makes a "hard" (never say "bad") case.

This doesn't only apply to litigation. Every lawyer needs all the facts to shape the advice she will give to her client. A transactional or business lawyer drafting a partnership agreement tallies the respective parties' intentions, obligations, capabilities, and plans. A trusts and estates lawyer learns everything there is to know about the assets in play, the identities of the prospective heirs, and the wishes of the client. A securities lawyer filing an initial public stock offering with the government masters the intimate details of the company issuing the stock.

Trust, but Verify

Psychology majors could have an inside track on this one: Clients don't always want to tell their lawyers the whole story. There are many possible reasons. The facts could be embarrassing, or "too personal." The client might not understand that they're relevant. Or, the

> *client could be hiding something wrong and think he's doing his lawyer a favor by keeping it covered up.*
>
> *Your job as a lawyer is to win the client's trust, probe him as far as possible, and, at this point, be that law school– trained skeptic. You have to go over the client's presentation of the facts for consistency and sense and maybe do a little gum-shoeing yourself to check things out.*
>
> *The client has to understand that hidden facts are almost certain to come out one way or another. You can only deal with them and give proper legal advice if you know them up front. In litigation, for example, if the last ones in court to learn the whole truth are you and the jury, there won't be much you can do about them by then.*

Sometimes lawyers get help in fact-gathering from paralegals and investigators. But it is the attorney who knows which facts matter. The lawyer is the only one who really understands how the legal issues come into play depending on the facts. A good lawyer knows how to get to the bottom of it all and is prepared to roll up the sleeves when necessary.

THE COUNSELOR

As mentioned above, facts either (1) are set in stone (appellate cases), (2) need development (fact investigation), or (3) are prospective (i.e., in the future). In this last case, the lawyer functions as a counselor— someone who advises the client how to proceed.

> **Good Counsel**
>
> *Being a "counselor" to a client means much more than dispensing legal information or even engaging in dispassionate legal analysis. Stanford Law School Dean Paul Brest believes that the counseling aspect of a lawyer's job makes for a relationship so close and ill-defined, that it presents attorneys with some substantial ethical dilemmas:*
>
> *Good lawyers . . . bring more to bear on a problem than legal knowledge and lawyering skills. They bring creativity, common sense, practical wisdom, and the most precious of attributes, good judgment.*
>
> *This description of the lawyer's role as counselor raises fundamental questions about the relationship between*

lawyer and client: When is the lawyer the independent actor or authority? When is he an agent subservient to the client's wishes? Is the relationship usefully understood as a partnership subject to ongoing negotiation? What are the lawyer's obligations when a client requests him to engage in actions that are lawful, but that he finds morally problematic because of their impact on others? What are his obligations when he believes that the client will use his analysis of the law to violate its spirit or even its letter? When he believes that the client is acting against her long-run self-interest?

At trial, lawyers sit at the "counsel table," and attorneys are frequently referred to as "counsellor" or "counsel." Remember the old favorite? "On the advice of counsel, I decline to answer that question on the grounds that it may tend to incriminate me." That means someone's giving good, and needed, counsel.

Thus, several skills are called upon here:

- The ability to listen
- Skills related to the non-legal advice
- Good judgment

THE ABILITY TO LISTEN

This goes back to the humility part. It's a bit of irony that lawyers, who in many places have what is politely called the "gift of gab," must shut the hell up to do their jobs well. Someone who doesn't listen is demonstrating that he doesn't care. His concern is with himself—showing off his knowledge, his expertise, his erudition, his eloquence.

A good lawyer listens, because he cares about his client and is willing to take his client's problem to heart. He needs to know the facts of the client's case, of course. But by listening closely and hearing between the lines, he can discern the client's true agenda and true needs.

Yet, at the same time, a lawyer must listen, and hear, at once sympathetically and *professionally*. Much as a physician, a good lawyer maintains the professional detachment necessary to render good counsel, even when his client's cause rouses him to the standard of "passionate advocacy." Even then, an attorney's craft demands that she maintain a just-so distance from the cause. She thus serves the client by properly counseling him as to what can realistically be accomplished. And she maintains her professional viability, ensuring that the matter she is being entrusted with is appropriate to her practice, economic situation, and competence.

NON-LEGAL SKILLS

There's a reason that most patent lawyers have scientific and engineering backgrounds. Any lawyer can learn the basics and finer points of patent law. But the only way to advise a client on what is required to make an invention patentable is to understand how the invention works, the "prior art" (the technology as it existed before the new invention), and the changes which might be necessary for the invention to qualify as unique enough to merit patent protection. The same goes for business and financial advice, and personal or psychological advice in a matrimonial context. Even a general practitioner who dabbles in many or all of these fields can't be an expert in all of them. American lawyers are traditionally more involved in non-legal advice-giving than many of their foreign counterparts.

But there is a limit. A lawyer understands how far her non-legal counsel extends. From that point on, she should get the next piece of advice from someone more knowledgeable or refer her client to another professional. And this gets us to the third fundamental skill in counseling: exercising good judgment.

GOOD JUDGMENT

Good judgment isn't born, it's created. (Some people, it's true, create it a lot faster than others.) It is perhaps the single most important quality a lawyer can bring to his practice. You may already possess the kind of judgment required of a lawyer, especially if you are older than a recent or soon-to-be college graduate, or you've had important non-academic responsibility or life experience.

To some extent, law school and the "legal analytic" method sharpen judgment. Mainly, however, good judgment is developed with practical experience and is honed by responsibility.

I Think Like a Lawyer, Therefore I Am

The much-trumpeted "learning to think like a lawyer" has its critics. It involves a process of socialization, even indoctrination. In its classical manifestation, law students are taught to remove their "selves" from the analytic process and apply an ostensibly objective "legal analysis."

One first-year student at Northwestern received a sharp reminder of this in a class discussion several years ago. Answering a question posed in a contracts class by then-Dean Robert Bennett, the student prefaced his opinion by saying, "Well, in my personal opinion . . ."

"Your personal opinion?" interjected Bennett, albeit with a smile. "We're not interested in your personal opinion."

The confused first-year gulped. Bennett continued: "Tell us your professional opinion." The idea Bennett wanted to get across was that a lawyer has to put aside his undisciplined "gut" feelings and intuitions. Instead, lawyers are supposed to attempt a dispassionate application of legal doctrine and analysis based on their reading of cases.

But another Chicago legal educator, Kent School of Law's Linda Hirschman, rejects the idea of the "cartesian self." That's the idea that a law student comes into law school with what the fictional Professor Kingsfield called "a head full of mush," or, as Descartes put it, a tabula rasa (blank slate). "It's utter nonsense," she says. "Many people go to law school and report that it was a devastating experience," she continues. The reason, she says, is the effect of "being told your views, thoughts, and experiences don't matter—being stripped of what they've already learned in college." She believes this process is harder on women, who are less inclined (because of their socialization, says Hirschman) to "wing it."

"It would help," she concludes, "if there were people like me in law school who say, 'You know, there isn't a cartesian Linda Hirschman, but I took a course in Utilitarianism and that's how I know this answer . . ."

It is a truism that all substantive decisions in a legal representation are to be made by the client: Should the settlement offer be accepted? Is this a sufficient price for the stock buyout? Is bankruptcy the right course to take?

Like most truisms, this one is hung up on the wall and given due deference, but it largely obscures the truth. Faced with the questions above, all but the most sophisticated or headstrong clients simply bounce them back and ask, "Well, what do you think?" Or, "You're being paid to counsel, so counsel." Ultimately the client is going to insist on knowing what you would do if you were in his place. He is entitled to know.

This prospect shouldn't panic you. As the years go by and your professional development continues, you'll come to welcome and seek out the exercise of judgment and discretion. Soon, except in the most massive and rigid giant firms or businesses, you'll find yourself with responsibilities that at one time you scarcely thought possible. If you're prepared eventually to take on that responsibility, it will come to you. In turn, you'll excel as a lawyer, and you'll love your work.

BIG-PICTURE PEOPLE

As part of their counseling function, lawyers are problem solvers and decision makers. They cut through the conceptual grease and grime to determine what the problem really is and what can be done about it. As Dean Brest puts it:

"A client often comes to a lawyer without a clear sense of his underlying objectives or interests, but with his mind fixed on a particular solution. The client may mistake the symptoms for the problem itself, define the problem too narrowly, or define it in terms of the most obvious or traditional solution. A good lawyer can assist clients in articulating their problems, defining their interests, ordering their objectives, and generating, assessing, and implementing alternative solutions."

Doing all that, says Brest, requires "multifaceted problem-solving and decision-making skills." That means having the capacity to handle the whole situation.

SOLUTIONS AND DECISIONS

Clients come to lawyers to solve their problems, problems that they believe have a legal aspect to them. Usually they're right—there is a legal element. But that element may be beside the point of the real problem.

A typical situation is where a businessman approaches a lawyer for "legal advice" on a joint endeavor in which he is involved. He wants to know what he has to tell his partners about another business venture he's involved in, how he can make sure his partner isn't squandering partnership opportunities or diverting them to himself, and who's allowed to hold on to the company checkbook. His litany of questions technically have legal answers.

But an insightful lawyer hearing the questions sees something the client isn't willing to tell himself. The real problem is that the client doesn't trust his partners, and his partners don't trust him.

Unless the issues that are driving them apart can be identified and repaired—perhaps through the use of a legal or law-related device that improves trust, such as requiring in the partnership agreement that both parties have the right to see the books at anytime—the petty issues of who's entitled to what are irrelevant. The client is, of course, entitled to the answers to his questions. But his attorney should be able to help him understand that the client can "pay me now or pay me later," meaning that on the present course a breakup is almost inevitable. He must advise the client about how to unwind the partnership, or otherwise extract himself from the doomed relationship, before the situation gets worse.

Blessed are the Peacemakers

Reconciling warring partners, be it in matrimony or business, can be tricky. Yet it is a service that most lawyers provide for their clients, since it is a form of avoiding the expense, risk, and aggravation of litigation.

The problem is, in a business dispute for example, that the lawyer may be opening herself up to losing both partners as potential clients, as well as the partnership. If both have reposed trust in her in the reconciliation process, she may be rendered ineligible to represent either in a dispute between them. If indeed there is a legal dispute, the partners should have separate counsel.

The up side, of course, is that she may salvage a valuable business client by getting the feuding factions to work things out.

Chances are the client expects his lawyer's advice on the non-legal stuff as well. This may be because the client, simply seeking succor, dumps the problem in her lap. Or because the subtleties between what is legal and what is financial, political, technical, or personal are lost in the many details of the problem. Or because the lawyer actually has special expertise in the associated non-legal field in which counsel is needed. And that's why they call them "counselors."

And Don't Spell it "Council"

Technically, a lawyer-as-counselor is a "counsellor" with two "ll"s. Lawyers merit more letters than guidance and camp counselors, and even today where you see the term "counsellor at law" it will be spelled this way. (In some states "counsellors at law" were once a special designation for attorneys with certain qualifications.) A lawyer is also in the literal sense a plain old "counselor": someone who imparts experience and advice.

THE ADVOCATE

A legal advocate is his client's face to the world. Advocacy involves three interrelated concepts:

- Representation
- Communication
- Negotiation

Representation

A lawyer representing her client is obligated to act solely in the client's best interests. While on duty, she is an agent—an instrument of her client. The only interests besides those of the client that she may consider are legal ethics, a topic beyond our discussion here. The main point is that her own interests must be put aside while she acts in the representative capacity.

Communication

This aspect of advocacy was addressed in the discussion in chapter 1 about a lawyer's need to be able to express himself clearly and effectively.

The lawyer-representative communicates the client's point of view not merely as well as the client, but better. To his role as advocate he brings his mastery of the facts and passion for the cause, plus legal knowledge, analytical skill, and personal eloquence.

Save It for Your Mom

Powerful oratory and dramatic courtroom histrionics may be impressive, but they're not always effectual. Experienced trial lawyers tell the story of the juror who approached the losing attorney after a trial. The juror said, "We really wanted to give it to you, because you were so good! You were really effective, but we couldn't do it." Of course, despite the "compliment," the lawyer wasn't effective at all. Certainly not for his client.

Negotiation

Negotiation is not "winning through intimidation"—though that may well be what serves the client best. But how many people can really win through intimidation each time out? And is "winning" always the goal?

The contemporary definition of negotiation is "collaborative problem-solving," according to Paul Brest. It's a modern, sum-sum approach to working things out between two or more parties. The idea, he writes, is "to identify and maximize the parties' interests—to expand the pie rather than divide it up."

Some people are natural negotiators, as demonstrated every day in flea markets, used-car lots, and cults. Others have to overcome a desire to get along at any price to negotiate effectively. Still others find that, while they are loath to "haggle" in their personal lives, they find it easier when doing it on behalf of a client. The role of representative enables them to avoid the exposure to personal offense that makes negotiation difficult. "You're right," they can now say, "but darn it, my client just won't agree to it. What can I do?"

Every lawyer negotiates, though some more than others. The skills of negotiation build on a lawyer's ability to work with people, his talent for communication and persuasion, and, as most other things, his reasoning and analytical skills. Again, there are also ethical issues in negotiation, which is a topic beyond the scope of this book. But they're probably not too hard for you to identify if you've ever been in a flea market, used-car lot, or cult.

THE GRAND DESIGN

Finally, lawyers must have vision. Once they've analyzed (taken apart) the problem or situation presented to them, they synthesize (put together) a solution. In the process, they add value from all the other necessary attributes we've discussed, not least of which being their knowledge of substantive law.

Applying legal knowledge, common sense, and imagination to a problem, the kinds of things lawyers design include:

- transactions
- organizations
- settlements
- trial strategies
- compensation programs
- corporate procedures
- "preventive legal care"

The skills necessary to be a "legal architect" are developed mostly through the knowledge of the existing patterns of how things are done in the respective specialties and the imagination to conceive of something that's never been done quite that way before.

In fact, it is in this area—the application of vision and imagination to helping people and organizations with their legal needs—that the best lawyers distinguish themselves. And it is one of the most enjoyable areas of legal work, too. When you can lift your head up from the routine, often numbing day-to-day work that is part and parcel of being a lawyer (especially in your early years in practice), being able to apply creativity is the breath of fresh air that makes it seem worth it.

CHAPTER FOUR

Where the Lawyers Are

"Lawyer" is a job title. But it tells you no more about what the person holding the title does with his day than does the title "business person." Even among those prelaw students most committed in theory to becoming lawyers, few really know what that commitment means in practice. Most law students think of the legal world as divided into big law firms and public-interest work. It's not. Indeed, even most attorneys, engrossed in their own work and its subculture, know little of the vast scope of their own profession.

By the same token, many who think that they would not want to practice law, despite having the talents, personality, and basic skills that would make it a good career choice for them, don't really know what they're passing up. Their image of what a lawyer really does is based on personally knowing one or two lawyers, images from Hollywood or television, or nothing much at all.

This chapter describes the most typical work environments for lawyers. It isn't necessary that you know what kind of lawyer you want to be before signing up for law school. People change specialties even during their careers. (Chapter 5 discusses the substantive work lawyers do in their respective specialties.)

But between these two chapters, and what's already been discussed thus far, you'll begin to form a realistic picture of the career options ahead of you, past the bland sign that says "lawyer." Besides developing a realistic idea of what a lawyer can be, these chapters will also provide a foundation for later chapters on choosing your undergraduate studies and deciding upon a law school suited to your career goals.

Private Practice

Most law school admissions offices gear their students toward private practice. That's where most of the jobs are, and that's where the best money is. In other words, most law schools gear their students toward jobs that will improve the schools' placement statistics.

In fact, the majority of lawyers are in private practice, and in all probability this will never change. Thus, according to the National Association for Law Placement (NALP), at least 50 percent of law school graduates have gone into private practice within six months of graduation in every year since the NALP started keeping track (1974).

A Little More Private

The National Association for Law Placement reports that while 55 percent of 1994 law school graduates accepted jobs in private practice, this represented the sixth straight year of decline from the 1988 high of over 64 percent. (See chapter 5 for a discussion of the economics of the legal economy.)

Small firms (2–25 attorneys) are the single largest source of employment for new graduates, employing nearly half of law school graduates entering private practice. In the last few years, only about a tenth of those entering private practice (or about 2,000 of the 40,000 or so total law graduates) entered firms of 251 or more.

Lawyers in private practice are members or employees of law firms, including firms of one lawyer (sole practitioners). Law firms generate income primarily through the charging of fees to private clients in return for providing legal services. There are, traditionally, two kinds of lawyers at law firms: partners and associates.

Partners and Associates

Partners are the "members" of the firm. (In some states firms are professional corporations or professional associations, as opposed to partnerships, and their members may be referred to as "shareholders," "directors," or the like.) Associates are their employees. In the traditional scheme, associates who prove themselves work their way up to partnership. This process typically could take five or six years, although today, partnership tracks of eight to ten years are common in medium- and large-sized firms.

Sometimes lawyers are affiliated with a law firm without being partners or associates. The most common title for such people is "of counsel" or just "counsel." Frequently, such people are senior but are not interested in maintaining a full-time law practice or are getting acquainted with the firm before being offered a partnership. In the case of large firms, these are frequently positions offered to associates who are still valuable to the firm but not valuable enough to be offered partnership.

TIME IS MONEY

Though there are exceptions, lawyers in private practice tend to make the most money in the profession. At the very top are starting salaries for major firms in New York, the country's richest and biggest legal market. First-year associates in these firms, which typically have 150 to 400 lawyers, make around $85,000. Partners in these firms average anywhere from $300,000 to $1.5 million or more per year. (In smaller cities, such as Chicago and Los Angeles, starting salaries at the biggest firms are closer to $65,000. In Philadelphia, salaries start at closer to $50,000.)

Pyramid Scheme

While it's nice for mid-senior partners in big firms to be compensated at, say, $300 an hour, there's a limit to how much money you can make selling your own time. You'd have to work a full two-thousand hours a year to gross $600,000. Pay your Park Avenue rent and your secretaries and your other expenses, and you're lucky if you clear a third of that. What's the use? Better to have worker ants gathering food (billable time) to feed the queen (the partnership) as much as possible.

The queen-partnership reigns in two ways. Rainmakers, of course, are partners who bring new clients to the firm. Thus they keep many worker ants busy billing time. Other partners have the ability to supervise many ants in vast projects and are similarly valuable. How valuable is it to keep a worker ant working? A first-year without even bar admission can be "billed out" at well over $100 an hour. Associate rates then proceed to around $200 an hour for the most experienced.

A rainmaker doesn't need giant cases. It's enough to keep one associate busy for six months, with, say, 10 to 20 percent of a mid-level partner's time, plus 5 percent of the rainmaker's time over ten, twenty, or more cases. It adds up.

By this system, known as "leverage," the queen-partnership can net $600,000 a year per person, or $800,000, or a million and a half or more (as at the richest large New York firms). An ant colony may look like a hill to you, but it's really a pyramid.

And a top time-billing associate is a top worker ant. Star ants bill twenty-three hundred hours a year, though many push three thousand. The typical "target" at major firms is two thousand hours. If you take the standard four weeks' vacation you're entitled to, two thousand hours a year is less than forty-two billable hours a week. That doesn't sound hard. For some people, it isn't. But you'd be amazed how tough hours forty-one through fifty can get.

But there are precious few starting jobs in such firms, as opposed to the nearly 40,000 people who graduate with J.D.s. With some exceptions, these positions are reserved for graduates of the top five or so schools or law-review editors and honor students at other schools in the top twenty, and regional schools.

In fact, according to NALP, only one in seven 1994 graduates who went into private practice reported salaries above $70,000. The average starting salary for 1994 law graduates in private practice was $50,000, but medians (averages) are a funny thing: A few high numbers can throw them off. In reality, nearly 40 percent of those going into private practice were getting paid $40,000 or less.

Not surprisingly, lawyers in private practice work the hardest. In the larger firms (and the not-so-giant firms in big cities) associates are usually required to work at least 2,000 hours a year of "billable" time. In the very largest firms, the typical associate might bill more like 2,400, with 3,000-hour billers not being unheard of.

But, as with most things, money can usually be traded readily for time. You can take a private practice job paying half the New York starting salary and be expected to bill perhaps 1,800 hours a year or even less.

SIZE AND SPECIALTY

The largest law firms are almost invariably "full service" firms, with departments handling virtually all the kinds of work discussed in the second section of this chapter. As firms get smaller, they tend to get more specialized, usually working in one or two of those areas. Smaller firms tend to have smaller work, in the sense of cases, transactions, and other matters involving less money. They usually are less profitable than larger firms, though there are many exceptions.

But there are some smaller firms, known as "boutiques," made up of alumni of large firms who take a key client or two with them and set up on their own. Boutiques have the culture of big firms (though they often claim not to), handle large matters, and typically pay salaries more in line with large firms.

GOVERNMENT

In private practice there is often the opportunity for great variety in the kind of work that comes your way. In government, the variety is more in the kind of work you choose, though once you get there the workload is fairly predictable. There are, however, many different work environments within the rubric of "government work." These include:

- Prosecutors' offices
- The U.S. Department of Justice
- Regulatory agencies
- The judiciary

The average starting salary in government work as reported by NALP is something less than $33,000. Years of government service can result in salaries that reach into the low six figures. Fringe benefits for government employees are legendary, not the least of which is their holiday schedule.

PROSECUTORS' OFFICES

If you want to do trial work, there are few places to get better experience than in a prosecutor's office. Working as a prosecutor is also a great way to get into public life. Plus, you get a badge, and most jurisdictions throw in a free leather carrying-case. But experiences in this field can be quite diverse, depending on where you work.

United States Attorney's Office

The most "desirable" (that is, the most prestigious and well-paying) prosecutor positions are as Assistant U.S. Attorneys. (Each federal judicial circuit has its own U.S. Attorney, appointed personally by the President.) These are the prosecuting jobs that pay best, are the most prestigious, and have the best resources at their disposal. The work is regular, but typically not 'round-the-clock. AUSAs work near the federal courthouses in their judicial district.

Traditionally, AUSAs prosecute relatively high-profile offenses, such as white-collar crime, grand larceny, and kidnapping. An increasing number of AUSAs have expressed dissatisfaction in recent years, however, as Congress has made more and more "less-interesting" offenses federal crimes. The federal courts are looking more and more like state courts, as drug runners, car-jackers, and other petty offenders are now federal cases.

There are also "Special AUSAs." These are assigned to different government agencies, such as the Internal Revenue Service or the Environmental Protection Agency. Their cache is not quite the same as those who work directly in the U.S. Attorney's office. But the training they receive is excellent preparation for private practice in their respective areas of specialty.

Few people are given the opportunity to go work in a U.S. Attorney's office straight out of law school. Their ranks are mostly made up of lawyers with a few years' experience as litigators in the best-regarded firms.

State Attorney Generals' and County Prosecutors' Offices.

These are the people who prosecute "everyday" crimes. Nomenclature may change from state to state, but typically junior lawyers in the Attorney General's office are "Deputy Attorneys General"; in the counties, they're "Deputy Prosecutors." Frequently, groups of state deputies are assigned to different sections or departments of state government, much like the AUSAs.

Achieving a Plurality

One is called an attorney general; two are attorneys general. It's a little like brothers-in-law. The reason? They're not "generals," as in military commanders. The noun (which takes the plural) is, of course, "attorney"; general is an adjective. (It's the same as "Surgeon General," though, thankfully, there's never more than one of them.) Think of it as if the title were "General Attorney," which it would be if the Normans who took over England in 1066 hadn't spoke French. But they did, especially in legal matters. While you're at it, and for the same reason, you can sound like a pro when referring to more than one military court proceeding: Those are courts martial.

Their work environments depend on the wealth and political situation of the states or counties where they're located. Some urban prosecutors work very long hours, mostly because they're overburdened with cases. Other prosecutors have a relatively leisurely lifestyle.

One negative side is that prosecutors, especially the hardest-pressed urban ones, often feel cynical about their jobs. Plea bargaining, uninterested judges, and unsupportive communities can make their jobs very difficult and trying.

But in terms of day-in, day-out trial experience and early responsibility, these jobs can't be beat. County prosecutors fresh out of law school can look forward to trying felony cases within a few years. As stepping stones to private practice, prosecutors' trial experience is highly regarded—but mostly in smaller firms that actually try cases. In contrast, the fancy "litigation departments" of the largest and most prestigious firms, which hardly ever actually try cases, are usually more interested in AUSAs than county prosecutors.

Justice Is Done

Special mention is due to the United States Department of Justice. While the respective U.S. Attorneys are in charge of "fighting crime" in their respective federal districts, "Justice" (as it's known) looks at the big picture. Its role is described by Congress in the following lofty terms:

[The Department of Justice] represents the interests of the nation and its citizens in the prosecution of all Federal criminal actions and civil actions taken to the Supreme Court. [It] ensures healthy competition in business, protects the nation from illegal immigration and drug trade, and renders legal advice to the President and the heads of the executive departments.

It kind of makes you want to salute.

Lawyers at Justice are assigned to various divisions, offices, and sections. Some sound suspiciously irrelevant to "justice," but rest assured that the offices are crawling with lawyers all the same. Their names will give you an idea of what they're about. (A brief description follows where elucidation might be helpful.):

- Drug Enforcement Administration
- Federal Bureau of Investigation
- Executive Office for U.S. Trustees (bankruptcy monitors)
- Community Relations Service
- Immigration and Naturalization Service
- Antitrust Division
- Civil Division (represents the U.S., its departments and agencies, Members of Congress, Cabinet officers, and other Federal employees when named as defendants in suits)
- Civil Rights Division
- Criminal Division (formulates criminal law enforcement policy and prosecutes some criminal law violations)
- Environment and Natural Resources Division (federal environmental litigation)
- Tax Division (tax litigation other than in Tax Court, which the IRS handles)
- Office of Special Counsel for Immigration-Related Unfair Employment Practices

Most Justice Department lawyers work in Washington, D.C., although there are regional offices.

Regulatory Agencies

As mentioned above, regulatory agencies such as the Environmental Protection Agency have their own Special AUSAs and other attorneys charged with enforcement. Other such agencies include the Occupational Health and Safety Administration, the Food and Drug Administration, the Federal Trade Commission, and basically any area where the government watches over some activity. These lawyers work in Washington, D.C. and in the respective judicial districts, or in some cases administrative "regions" throughout the country.

And for every federal agency there is usually a state agency (albeit not every agency is replicated in every state) that also has a slew of lawyers working for it, usually in the state capitols and major cities within the state. Most attorneys working in government work for state and local governments. Pay is somewhat better with the feds.

Note that in both the federal and state cases, this work is often not criminal prosecution. Regulation doesn't always involve criminal charges. Some regulatory lawyers act as gatekeepers, advising the government and the public when regulations are being complied with and making recommendations on developing regulation. Some agencies don't have their own criminal prosecution apparatus at all and refer potential criminal violations, or even civil litigation, to the U.S. Attorney or the Department of Justice (see below).

D.C. Currency

If you'd asked Lee Walzer where he wanted to be after law school, the last place he would have mentioned was the Office of the Comptroller of the Currency, one of the agencies that regulates the banking industry. He hadn't even heard of it.

"I thought because of my multilingual background that I would do 'international law,'" says Walzer, a 1988 graduate of Northwestern who speaks French and Hebrew. "But that doesn't really exist as a field, independent of corporate and litigation work."

Walzer did know he liked Washington, where earlier he had spent time as an intern. At Northwestern's career-planning orientation, he signed up for whatever government employers were interviewing on campus. "I knew nothing about the Comptroller of the Currency. But the woman who interviewed me was really interesting, and we really hit it off," he says. "I got here in the middle of the savings and loan crisis. It's remained interesting as the financial services industry has gone through a lot of change." His agency's job, says Walzer, is to help the industry keep up with change while staying within legislative limitations on what banks may do.

Did his political science background provide adequate preparation for the job? Not really. "I had to learn tons," he answers, noting that he took a banking law seminar in the spring after he took the job, "but I really learned by doing."

On the other hand, there is lots of non-criminal litigation out there in government work. Many regulatory bodies, such as the ones enumerated above, are empowered to bring civil actions against those who stray across legal lines. In many respects, these actions are similar to what you might do in a law firm, except you'll have more responsibility than in private practice. You'll also have virtually limitless resources (especially if you work for the feds) to call well-polluters, tax-evaders, and package-mislabelers to task. Other regulatory legal jobs, however, may be poorly funded.

LEGAL OFFICES OF OTHER DEPARTMENTS AND AGENCIES

Just as every business has a lawyer, every government body has a lawyer, or ten. Here are just some of the kinds of positions for lawyers in government not addressed above:

- **Corporation counsel**—The "in-house" law firm for larger cities, in their "corporate" sense. They deal with the city's property, financial holdings, and defend the city in civil litigation.

- **G-Person**—The FBI (a branch of Justice) and the Secret Service (a branch of the Treasury—isn't there something scary about the IRS's police being called the Secret Service?) are filled with Special Agents who are lawyers. Yeah, they get guns.

- **Legislative offices**—Most legislators have at least one lawyer in their office who assists in evaluating and drafting legislation, as well as other legal issues that arise. Big shots, especially those who chair important committees and subcommittees, have several attorneys at their beck and call.

- **Executive counsel offices**—The President, and most state governors, have their own in-house lawyers as well. Some of our leaders are able to keep quite a few of these busy. There are also counselors for others in the executive branch, such as secretaries of departments and the like. These tend to be higher-paying positions and are, not surprisingly, reserved for very experienced people.

THE JUDICIARY

There are two main areas of interest for lawyers working in the judicial branch of government: judges and law clerks.

Judges

It's good to be the judge in the same way that it's good to be the king. Judges have tremendous power, especially federal judges, who are appointed by the President of the United States and, upon confirmation by Congress, are approved for life. Most state judges are appointed, though many are elected, and often only for limited terms.

Judges are the human embodiments of the judicial branch of government. This is why they're formally called "the court," as in, "If I may address the court." Obviously, only experienced attorneys could conceive of running for a judicial seat. The pay can be good, getting into the low six-figures. Yet most federal judges are so accomplished professionally that accepting appointment to the federal bench may involve a 50 to 70 percent pay cut in regions where law firms are most profitable.

State court judges generally come in these different sizes:

- **Municipal court judges** are usually not full-time judges at all but prominent local attorneys "moonlighting" in black robes. The prosecutors in municipal court are also usually regular attorneys by day and are appointed or elected to their positions, often as entree into local politics.

- **Lower Court judges,** besides those in municipal court, are usually full-time judges who preside over landlord-tenant or housing courts, small-claims courts, city courts (the equivalent of municipal judges but with enough work to keep them busy full time), and night courts.

- **Trial Court judges** preside over the main trial courts in most states. (In New York, trial court judges are called Supreme Court judges, and that state's highest court is called the Court of Appeals. Other states call the trial court "Superior Court," "County Court," or various other names.)

- **Appellate judges** sit on the intermediate courts of appeal—the body that decides appeals from the superior courts. Most cases don't get higher than this.

- **Supreme Court** judges are the top dogs in their respective states. Theirs is the last word on the interpretation of state laws, the constitutionality of state law under the state constitution, and the regulation of the state bar.

The federal court system has these main gradations:

- **United States Magistrates** are named for fixed terms. They handle certain administrative tasks when cases are first filed and also supervise pretrial discovery— the part of a civil case where the sides have to turn over relevant information to their adversaries. Parties may agree to have a magistrate try a case; though they have a constitutional right to a District Court judge, they may save years off the waiting time necessary to get one.

- **United States District Judges** are appointed for life. They try the cases, issue the orders, make the calls.

- **United States Circuit Court Judges** are the intermediate-appellate court judges in the federal system. They're almost inevitably the last word on a case.

- **United States Supreme Court Judges** have the ultimate say-so on whether a law is constitutional and what federal laws mean. There are only nine of them at a time. Very few people go from this job to any other employment. (To the contrary, William Howard Taft went from President to Chief Justice of the United States.)

There are other, specialized, federal judges as well, in the following courts:

- U.S. Bankruptcy Court
- U.S. Court of Federal Claims (for suits against the government)
- U.S. Tax Court
- U.S. Court of International Trade

Also, there are untold minions of Administrative Law Judges (ALJs) in both the state and federal systems. ALJs preside over hearings by regulatory agencies, which are usually considered "quasi-judicial," such as disputes over Social Security or other benefits. Procedural rules are more relaxed in these courts than in the formal court systems. That isn't to say, however, that ALJs don't wield a lot of power.

Depending on where they sit, judges' workloads vary. Again, government budgets make all the difference. And many federal courts are overwhelmed largely as a result of slow congressional action over nominees to the federal bench, whose approval would result in less backlog.

There are those who find that being a judge is difficult, because the social problems they face are great and there is so little that they can do about them. But judicial positions are highly sought-after. Judges can make a big difference in the world, and there's nothing more prestigious in the profession.

LAW CLERKS

This isn't *exactly* a job. At least, it's not a career. But it's a place you might want to find yourself after law school. The top students at various schools (usually so determined by their membership and leadership on the law review) serve as clerks for appellate and supreme court judges. At the trial level, at least in the state courts, these positions are more readily available to those with less gilded credentials.

Law clerks are like associates for judges. They do the research, and much of the writing, for the opinions issued the judges issue. The main thing they do, though, is mark their calendars for the end of their one- or two-year clerkships. At the end, they are inevitably offered positions in the top law firms. Or they may be elevated to higher clerkships (the Supreme Court only takes former Circuit Court clerks for its own clerks), from where they may go on to virtually any elite position—the top government and private jobs, or the faculties of top law schools. Many Supreme Court clerks end up as judges themselves.

GOOD ENOUGH FOR GOVERNMENT WORK

You'll never know if you'd like to be a government lawyer if you don't know just how widely the government spreads its beneficent net. Here's a list of some of the places lawyers work in the Federal government alone. (Remember, most government lawyers work for state and local governments.) It's mostly limited to cabinet-level departments and free-standing government "establishments" and corporations. Each one of these has lots of little departments where lawyers can be found, though, and special mention is made of notable colonies:

Executive Branch Departments

- Department of Agriculture
- Department of Commerce
    Patent and Trademark Office
- Department of Defense
    Defense Contract Administration Services
- Department of Education
- Department of Energy
- Department of Health and Human Services
    Social Security Administration
    Food and Drug Administration
- Department of Housing and Urban Development
    Federal Housing Commission
- Department of the Interior

- *Department of Justice (see text)*
- Department of Labor
    Solicitor of Labor's office
- Department of State
- Department of Transportation
- Department of the Treasury
    Bureau of Alcohol, Tobacco and Firearms
    Office of the Comptroller of the Currency
    United States Customs Service
    Federal Law Enforcement Training Center
    Internal Revenue Service
    Office of Thrift Supervision

Selected Independent Establishments and Government Corporations

- Central Intelligence Agency
- Commission on Civil Rights
- Consumer Product Safety Commission
- Environmental Protection Agency
- Equal Employment Opportunity Commission
- Federal Communications Commission
- Federal Deposit Insurance Corporation
- Federal Election Commission
- Federal Labor Relations Authority
- Federal Mediation and Conciliation Service
- Federal Trade Commission
- General Services Administration
- National Labor Relations Board
- National Mediation Board
- Nuclear Regulatory Commission

- Occupational Safety and Health Review Commission
- Office of Government Ethics
- Office of the Special Counsel
- Resolution Trust Corporation
- Securities and Exchange Commission
- United States Postal Service

This list is unlikely to shrink, regardless of who's in Congress and the White House. But there's a chance that entirely new fields of government employment will open up. After all, in the early 1980s no one dreamed how many lawyers would be supported by the practice of rehabilitating savings and loans.

GOVERNING PRINCIPLES

All told, there's lots of government work for the willing attorney. It's generally considered a more civilized lifestyle than private practice, and, again, people never stop talking about the fringe benefits. It's also fairly stable, if you get in.

On the other hand, Government hiring tends to be streaky, depending on political and macroeconomic conditions (read: budget deficits). Some state governments are in a perpetual hiring freeze, though it's said that the right word from the right contact can thaw out a spot from time to time. And the work is often fairly routine in a given position.

Finally, you'll never get rich as a civil servant—unless you're able to sell your government experience in the private-practice market. But while that might sound good, making it happen requires unusually good foresight into what specialties will be in demand years from now. Some people get very lucky this way, but others languish in their civil-service law jobs as the years turn into decades. But wow—what a pension!

CORPORATE / IN-HOUSE

Employment as a lawyer for a corporate legal department can be an ideal compromise between the demands of firm practice and the limited opportunity in government. In-house lawyers have a chance to soar to the top of business leadership. But in-house work can also merely be a lower-paying law firm job in a place where partnership is literally impossible.

The best in-house jobs are those offered to experienced attorneys, those who usually have a few years (sometimes as many as twenty) under their belt. These positions often involve the management of outside law firms, which requires experience but not necessarily all that much exertion. People working in these contexts are often just one of a handful of lawyers at the company. They are basically business executives, managers of an outsourced service. Often they report to top management—or they are top management, with a title such as Vice President for Legal Affairs. Compensation in such positions can be quite generous, with bonus schedules unheard of in law firms, and the lifestyle can be fantastic.

Similar positions are those that are not so much management of outside counsel (typically in litigation matters), but real in-house legal work, mostly in the transactions area. Many lawyers who gain experience in corporate transactions—mergers and acquisitions, finance, business planning—are eager to be principals instead of agents. In-house positions such as this, typically found in entrepreneurial environments, are often tickets to direct management of a company.

PET LAW FIRMS

The flip side of in-house work is companies with law departments that employ scores or even hundreds of lawyers. These are essentially law firms that happen to be in-house. Such positions are the ones most often available to recent law school graduates. Pay is usually lower than for a comparable law firm job—a median of $42,000 a year in 1994, compared to the $50,000 for first-years in private practice. For people hired after a few years in a firm, salaries may initially be higher than in the last job, but with little up side. Benefits are usually superior than those available to lawyers in firms.

Though the lifestyle in a big corporate law department can be much better than private practice, the opportunities are usually more limited. And in many such departments, whips have been known to be cracked. The same need to increase productivity found in law firms can rear its head in a corporate law department. In such contexts, lawyers accustomed to the collegiality of law firm life (even in modern times) may be chagrined to find themselves called to discuss their "outplacement," not with a senior lawyer or an executive, but a personnel manager in Human Resources.

LEGAL EDUCATION

Chapter 1 discusses some aspects of becoming a law professor. Frankly, this option is available to very, very few. Law teaching is a desirable position, and the competition is fierce. Though there are exceptions everywhere, by and large law professors are recruited from the graduates of the top schools in the country, and inevitably from people who have served in prestigious judicial clerkships.

TEACHING LAW: EXTENDED COCOON TIME

Some lawyers only come into their full intellectual strength when the callowness of youth is past. Is there any hope to get back onto the hot-shot track and make a run at something like law teaching?

It is possible, at least for those who were in the right league in the first place. Some judges, including Federal District Court judges, will consider clerkship applications from students who have been in practice at well-regarded firms for two or three years. People who may not have made law review, but can point to subsequent accomplishments (ideally, a published article or two), may thus get another chance. It also doesn't hurt if you can strike up a relationship with such a judge while litigating a case in her courtroom.

A District Court clerkship can, if you want it badly enough, possibly lead to a Circuit Court clerkship, the stuff law school appointments are made of. Again, someone trying such a tack must make the commitment to write and get published, even though published work is not usually expected of recent clerks.

Another approach is to add a graduate degree. Some schools offer advanced law degrees, such as the LL.M., but these are usually for specialization in practice (typically in tax). Other advanced law degrees, such as the LL.D, Doctor of Laws, may be more useful. It may be worthwhile for someone who really wants to make this happen to get an advanced degree in another discipline, then find some cross-disciplinary way to present this accumulated scholarship to a law school. This would require a very large investment in time; the better part of a decade for a Ph.D. But it demonstrates that, for those who came close and regret barely missed opportunities, repentance is possible.

PUBLIC INTEREST

Whether you think today's politically correct cause is actually incorrect, or if you think it's the embodiment of rectitude, public interest law will still have the same definition: Lawyers working for non-profit organizations supported by donations or, perhaps, government grants.

There is a widespread belief in the bar—and especially in the judiciary—that all lawyers are obligated to work *pro bono publico*, "for the public good." (See sidebar.) But people who commit themselves to public interest law take that a step further. Frequently, they are qualified enough to be able to command salaries at other firms several times the pittances typically made available to public interest lawyers. Nonetheless, such people decide to apply their talents and skills directly to what they regard as the betterment of humanity.

> *The argument in favor of mandatory pro bono is that there are serious legal needs not being met, and only lawyers can meet them. The argument against it is that there are serious food, shelter, and clothing needs not being met either, yet no one tells farmers, landlords, or clothiers to provide those things for free.*
>
> *There is a consensus, however, that being a professional includes some kind of public service obligation. Some large law firms have established "public interest fellowships," whereby one or more associates are "donated" to supervise pro bono work for six months or a year. The associates are paid a full salary and given all the support services normally available to attorneys working on firm matters, and don't lose seniority credit.*
>
> *Whatever the motivation, the programs are well-received both by the recipients of the legal services and the associates who get to provide it.*

You might think that there's plenty of work for people willing to take peanuts for their trouble. That's true if you want to serve private clients for free. But positions with established public interest groups are quite competitive. Notwithstanding the low pay, they provide a lot more job satisfaction than creating new and exciting forms of real estate syndications, or writing the perfect pretrial discovery request on behalf of a multinational behemoth.

> ### Public Interesting
>
> *"The most impressive thing to me," says Jane Golberg, former Assistant Director of the Legal Affairs Department of the Anti-Defamation League in New York, "was that I was surrounded by colleagues of such high caliber."*
>
> *Golberg, a 1987 graduate of Stanford, had spent a year wandering unhappily through a medium-sized corporate law firm in Manhattan when she realized it wasn't for her. During her last year of law school, she had worked as an intern at the ADL, one of the leading organizations monitoring and combating anti-Semitism. (She received a full semester's credit for her full-time work at ADL.) "I wanted to be happy," she said. "And I was so happy there."*

On the strength of her past work at ADL, she was invited for an interview. She got the job, which she kept and, she says, enjoyed for two years until moving on. "You would think jobs like this would be available for anyone, considering what they pay," she says. "But I was working with smart, accomplished people who could easily have worked wherever they wanted to."

HOW IT WORKS

Public interest law groups typically volunteer to represent individuals whom they believe are being unjustly prosecuted (e.g., for teaching Darwinian evolution to schoolchildren), bring suits in their names to secure certain rights (e.g., the right to an abortion), or represent all members of some class they maintain is injured (e.g., black children being denied admission to all-white public schools). They may also request permission from courts involved in litigation to submit *amicus curiae*, or "friend of the court" briefs in matters where they are neither counsel nor parties.

The best known public interest advocacy groups are, broadly speaking, liberal. They include the American Civil Liberties Union (ACLU), the Southern Poverty Law Center, the National Association for the Advancement of Colored People (NAACP), and the National Organization for Women (NOW).

But there's more than one political stripe among public interest lawyers. The last decade has seen the growth of conservative public-interest advocacy groups such as the Capital Legal Foundation, the Pacific Legal Foundation, and the Family Research Council. These and others have scored some important victories for their constituencies, such as property owners who object to having their land devalued by environmental regulations and advocates of attenuated forms of school prayer. These groups have added other points of view to the argument about "big" vs. "little" government and what may be deemed the "public interest."

CHAPTER FIVE

Specialties Are Our Specialty

One of the great things about the modern legal profession is that you may be able to practice law in an area related to other interests you have. The reason for this is that lawyers are required at many junctures in modern commerce, social intercourse, and even culture.

That isn't to say, however, that you can make a living at every specialty that interests you, or that you can even secure a position in them. For example, there are a lot of people who want to be rock and roll lawyers, sports lawyers, or multimedia lawyers, but of course not everyone can.

You can try, though. What follows is an introduction to the most popular legal specialties and some discussion of the kind of background that might help you get your foot in the door. As in the previous chapter, the information here goes into the bank for the later chapters on choosing courses and choosing law schools. And if you're still in the "undecided" category, this chapter should push you over the line, one way or another.

Not all the specialties described below are specialties unto themselves. Most are actually specialties of corporate (transactional) practice with occasional forays into litigation. Depending on the organization with which a lawyer practices, an individual area may be in a self-contained corporate law department—essentially, an in-house law firm. Or it may be that someone is just "the international law guy" in corporate law firm or "the intellectual property woman" in litigation.

LITIGATION

Why is litigation the dominant subject of TV lawyering? Probably because trials and cases are relatively action-packed, have moments of genuine drama, and seem to have a good guy and a bad guy. It's no surprise that applications to law school increased 15 percent the fall after "L.A. Law" debuted. Litigators are described by some as "the surgeons of law": blood, guts, glory, and arrogance—sounds about right.

To "litigate" is to turn to a court to resolve a dispute; "litigation" is a lawsuit. But getting a court involved is very different from actually having a trial, and that's the biggest difference between TV litigation and real life.

There is, in fact, something of a class/social breach in the civil practice bar between self-described "litigators" and self-described "trial lawyers" (see below), even if the distinction isn't always crystal clear. In reality, the difference between corporate "litigators" and "trial lawyers" is a bit artificial. There's a spectrum of cases and practices that fall between the mythical extremes. Any good trial lawyer can handle motion practice and paper discovery, and ultimately a good litigator must be able to try cases (or must have a partner who can). But drawing the extremes illustrates the variety of civil litigation practices.

LITIGATORS

Litigators usually work for larger firms doing larger cases. Most of these are business disputes. Though litigators rarely try cases, they are frequently involved with judges and adversaries. They mainly supervise and dicker over discovery, the process by which the two sides in a civil case go about exchanging information, as required by the law. Litigators do some criminal defense work. Usually it's white-collar (non-violent) litigation, involving lots of paper trails and little real action. Thus litigators "litigate" these cases more or less the same way they do contract disputes.

Litigators make loads of motions, which are requests of the court. Sometimes these are related to discovery; other motions are requests that the court dismiss the other side's case, or parts of it, because they don't hold water. Essentially, the side making such a motion says, "Even if everything the other side said were true, they still wouldn't be saying anything they have a legal right to recover for. Let's just go home."

Further down the road, litigators spend a lot of time on motions for "summary judgment." These are similar to motions to dismiss, but with facts thrown in. The side making a motion says, "Look judge, they've had years to find evidence of wrongdoing, and there's nothing in the record that supports their claims. No jury could possibly agree with their claims. Let's save time and money and throw this out before trial."

If a motion fails, litigators try cases. But their goal is to settle them, because at a trial the stakes and risks are high.

Litigation at the Big Firm

What is a big firm? "Big" is relative, of course. In major cities, firms are "big" if they have more than 100 lawyers. But culturally, they're not really big law firms until they crack 300, including one major office with at least, say, 200.

Big law firms provide highly sophisticated legal services to big companies. Most big companies are corporations, of course, hence the term, "corporate law firms." Corporate law firms provide several types of legal service, but they can basically be broken into the "corporate" or "transactional" areas, and litigation.

Most litigators work in large firms; refer to the previous chapter for the lowdown on their economic and lifestyle issues.

TRIAL LAWYERS

Trial lawyers, to continue the gross generalization, can't stand all the paper-pushing that litigators do. They want the jury to hear the facts and decide the merits of the case. Though they are often involved in business (contract) disputes, most self-described trial lawyers practice either criminal law or personal-injury and other negligence-related cases, known as torts.

A tort, broadly speaking, is any non-contractual wrong one person or business does to someone else either through carelessness or on purpose. It can also include something that a person's property "does" to someone else. An example might be an icy sidewalk where a person slips and sustains an injury. In court this person would try to prove that she had a reasonable expectation of being safe on that sidewalk. Lawyers who frequently handle torts can be called "tort lawyers," "personal injury" (or "P.I.") lawyers, or "negligence lawyers."

There are two sides (at least) to every tort, and one lawyer (at least) for every side. The practice of the plaintiff's lawyer—the one who represents the injured party—tends to be somewhat unpredictable. The main reason for this is that plaintiff-P.I. lawyers almost always work on a *contingency* basis. They keep a percentage of the award or settlement made to their client. If the client loses, the lawyer gets nothing for his trouble. A successful practice in this area, though, can be quite systematic, and the risks minimized by careful selection of cases.

The practice of the defendant's lawyer, however, is more stable, if somewhat less exciting. She almost invariably works for an insurance company; her firm might be what is called a "captive" insurance defense firm, which is all but an in-house firm. She bills by the hour, and because she is so specialized—and probably very capable considering she represents a client as prized as an insurance company—her hourly rate is a healthy one.

Except for times when he's actually "on trial," the insurance-defense lawyer's hours are usually somewhat regular. It doesn't hurt that she doesn't have to spend as much time marketing her wares as her adversary, who, while not an ambulance chaser, does have to keep her calling card in play.

CRIMINAL LAW

Under the Constitution, anyone charged with a crime has the right to a criminal defense lawyer. Some big firms do criminal work, but not like Perry Mason and Matlock. Big-firm criminal work is almost always "white collar" defense, that is, defending people not accused of violent crimes. This type of crime includes market manipulators, tax tricksters, bank busters, and securities swindlers.

White collar criminal litigation is a lot like civil litigation with a few differences: The government is one of the parties, it gets a big head start, it has an unlimited budget, and the rules are slanted in its favor.

As a potential criminal lawyer, you must come to terms with this reality: Your job *will* involve keeping people who have committed crimes from being punished for what they have done. No one in criminal defense work routinely turns down representations because they think the potential client may be guilty. That's a luxury for spectators.

The other side of the criminal law bar is peopled by prosecutors, whose work is discussed elsewhere. Most prosecutors go on to become criminal defense lawyers, often very frighteningly successful ones.

Ultimately, regardless of which side of the criminal law game you want to play, you must come to terms with just how high the stakes can be. Have you ever seen a grown man, head bowed before a judge, shackled at the wrists and ankles, with a sheriff's deputy at each of his elbows? Until you have, you can't really comprehend the stakes. It's a sobering vision.

Most members of the criminal defense bar are not in big firms. They often describe their practice as exhilarating, and in many ways you can't play closer to the edge than as a criminal lawyer. (Some play too close. Then they need their own lawyers.) The practice has its risks, however. You spend a lot of time hanging around with criminals, especially as you try to develop business.

Also, criminal defendants are often not among the best-heeled people, and collecting fees can be tricky—especially if you lose. But this is a profitable area in which to practice if your client has assets that have not been seized.

FAMILY LAW

Although most family lawyers end up in court at one point or another, and though their practical legal skills are much like those of litigators, they are a species unto themselves. One reason is that juries have nothing to do with family law disputes, which are decided entirely by judges. This discounts the value of showmanship and those other trial-lawyer-type attributes.

Family lawyers deal mainly with separation and divorce, and the issues that flow from these events, such as child custody, disposition of property (and tracing of assets, if necessary), interspousal violence and orders of protection, and just about any awful thing people who were once in love can perpetrate on each other. Some family lawyers also handle adoption proceedings.

As the field develops, and society evolves, family lawyers are being called on to stretch the way law reflects social mores. Thus, they are involved in cases that seek to enable same-sex couples to seek official sanction, employment benefits, and the right to adopt children. Sometimes they also find themselves in leading-edge cases involving surrogate parenting, adoptees' rights, and the like. If you want to be one of those people who push the envelope of social change, or, if you want to be one of those pushing back, this field could be for you.

A warning: Some of the disputes family lawyers find themselves involved in would drain the color from the most hardened criminal attorney's face. Because of the emotion involved, family law is an area where a lawyer can be remembered as an angel (often avenging), or a demon—especially when it comes time to collect that fee. It gets very personal.

CORPORATE (TRANSACTIONAL) LAW

Transactional work includes the formation and organization of business' entities, and the rendering of advice about which business form to utilize and where on earth to put it. Transactional lawyers (a firm's "corporate department") also make it possible to issue stock, merge, acquire or divest of entities or shares in them, and to conduct complex transactions among complex entities.

Technically, lawyers aren't necessary to *do* most of these things. The legal requirements, however, of complex securities, financial and corporate happenings are positively occult. Undertaking them without sophisticated legal counsel would be like performing your own appendectomy on the kitchen table. Millions or billions of dollars often hinge on the quality of the legal guidance that makes these happenings possible. Thus, it's not remarkable that the partners who render this advice charge rates of $300–$400 an hour or more.

Fishing for Efficiency

The classical way lawyers in private practice have been paid is by charging an hourly fee. Traditionally, the hour was broken into as many as ten increments of six minutes each, though increments as large as a quarter of an hour are used in some firms as well.

The hourly rate problem is obvious: The lawyer has no incentive to get the job done quickly, at least until the client's tolerance is pushed to the limit. After all, can anyone complain that her lawyer is "too thorough"?

The hourly rate, however, is dying something of a slow death. Clients have found the ideal way to change the lawyer's incentive: getting another lawyer. Gone are the

Corporate practice is as diverse as the kinds of commerce that take place. Not only corporations use "corporate" lawyers' services. Businesses—large, medium, and small—can be partnerships, limited partnerships, limited-liability companies, or sole proprietorships, not to mention non-profit organizations, a sub-specialty in corporate law unto itself. All these kinds of organizations need business lawyers at one point or another, although it is when these clients seek to raise capital by issuing stocks and bonds that the "corporate" lawyers perform some of their most important functions.

TRUSTS AND ESTATES/TAX

Morbid as it may sound, death and taxes make for excellent professional opportunities. There are actually two broad kinds of tax practice, though some tax lawyers practice in both of them. One is trusts and estates, which is helping people plan for the disposition of their property after death. The other is business tax practice, which is really a kind of corporate law. This specialty involves analyzing the tax consequences of certain business transactions. And, of course, there are many tax lawyers who work for the IRS or as tax court judges.

Trusts and estates lawyers work mostly on their own or in smaller firms. (They also exist in large, "full-service" firms, and are available at great expense for clients of the firms' other departments.) They analyze clients' assets and advise them of the best way to shield their life's work from taxes or even ill-advised dissipation by heirs. There are many devices available to achieve this, more than most other lawyers ever want to know.

Retirement and other financial planning often dovetails nicely with this work, and in fact many lawyers in trusts and estates started out as financial planners or insurance salespeople. Some observers think "T&E" will be one of the big-growth fields in law in the years to come. The ubiquitous baby boomers are thinking seriously about their retirement needs and even, immortal as they are, planning for subsequent generations.

All kinds of tax lawyers advise their clients in disputes with the IRS or state taxing authorities over interpretation of the tax law. (Someone who's up on criminal charges for tax evasion usually needs a litigator at this point.) Tax attorneys obviously include those who work for the IRS or state taxing authorities. Tax lawyers also work with non-profit groups to ensure that they maintain their tax-exempt status.

Tax law is one area for which, most attorneys agree, you really need "a certain kind of head." Some maintain that an undergraduate background in accounting or finance is a necessity in this field. There is virtually no area of law in which a specific undergraduate preparation is necessary, but if you have that "certain kind of head," maybe you're majoring in a related field anyway. Or maybe you don't even have to.

INTELLECTUAL PROPERTY

Once an obscure specialty, intellectual property—the protection of "intellectual," or abstract conceptual rights—is beginning to overwhelm other specialties, as computers and other technologies take their place as major engines of the world economy. It is now one of the most exciting areas of law and promises to grow and grow.

The idea of protecting intellectual property, such as patents and copyrights, is to give would-be inventors and developers an incentive to bring ideas to market. Patent and copyright holders are granted legalized monopolies on technologies or expressions of ideas. Trademark owners are not given a property right by the law, but the law protects their ability to use a certain mark, brand name, or package appearance to ensure consumers that they are buying a product that comes from the source they think it does.

PATENT LAW

Patent law is one of the few fields that requires a specific undergraduate background (science) in virtually every case. All the "gadgets" and "clever ideas" that non-scientists think of when they think of inventions have probably been patented. Now the action is in high technology: biotechnology, computing, electrical engineering, and allied fields. You simply have to understand this stuff to practice in this area.

In fact, patent law is the only specialty that has its own bar exam, in addition to the bar exam every law school grad needs to pass to be called a lawyer. But in the end, it pays off. This is a financially rewarding field, although its charms may not appeal to everyone. Patent lawyers are in great demand at law firms and in-house at technology companies. Some patent lawyers who represent impoverished inventors on a contingency basis and take a share of the royalties earned from the invention after it's patented and goes to market are the top earners in the profession. Patent litigation, which may be initiated when someone claims someone else is using a patented technology without permission (or "infringing") is also a highly-specialized area of practice, and potentially quite lucrative.

Most patent lawyers end up practicing in the allied fields of copyright and trademark, even though these don't necessarily require technical expertise.

Trademark

"Trade identity," which, as mentioned above, includes special names, symbols, packaging ("trade dress"), or even color combinations, assure consumers that they're getting what they think they're getting. If you want a Coke®, you look for that red-and-white bottle. As you can imagine, the trade identity of Coca-Cola® is one of the most valuable in the galaxy, which is why they like it when you put those little ®s after their name.

This symbol means that the words preceding it are "registered trademarks." They remind the reader that Coke® and Coca-Cola® are protected symbols. Companies that are lax in this matter often find their once-proud brand names becoming unprotectable "generic" words. Think of "cellophane." Think of "aspirin." Think, in fact, of "cola," one that the Coca-Cola® people let slip away about a hundred years ago.

Lawyers advise companies about protecting these rights, choosing names that don't interfere with the rights of others, and litigating disputes when the first two don't work. Wrongful use of someone else's trade dress is called infringement. Many litigators specialize in trade-dress–infringement litigation, which has its own specialized modes of proof and trial.

Unfair Competition

A related area is "unfair competition" law. Fundamentally, trademarks are a subset of "unfair competition" law, which is about protecting consumers from misunderstanding what they are doing with their money. But a business can be engaged in unfair competition without necessarily infringing a trademark if it's doing something that misleads consumers. An example would be making false health claims or false claims about a competitor's product.

There are various types of civil litigation that can arise from such practices, and they are affected by public law as well. Fair competition is regulated by the Federal Trade Commission, which can bring civil or criminal actions for such activities. So lawyers interested in this field may spend time at the FTC or may defend against FTC and related state regulatory actions in private practice.

COPYRIGHT LAW

Copyright law protects the owner of a unique, published expression from unauthorized reproduction of her work. Books, videos, TV shows, movies, software, and computer games are all made by people who have talent and have worked hard to develop ideas that people will buy. Unauthorized reproduction, which deprives creators of the fruit of their labor, is punishable by both civil and criminal law.

Licensing

Today's copyright lawyers do much more than file creator's works with the Library of Congress and get an automatic copyright (the © symbol). You don't need a lawyer to do that. Rather, they are engaged in helping creators and publishers get the most value from their copyrighted works. The main way of doing this is by licensing, which means giving others the right to use the material in a specified way for a royalty payment.

Licensing is also a big part of the trade-identity practice. Brand-name logos and characters from movies and TV are protected by trademark and copyright, sometimes both. These images are licensed to producers of coffee mugs, T-shirts, and all those other awful things in return for a royalty.

What if someone makes or sells a product with a protected design on it without permission? Finding and prosecuting those who trade in these unlicensed counterfeits or "knock-offs," both civilly and criminally, is another sub-specialty within intellectual property and litigation.

INTERNATIONAL LAW

Old Richard Daley, the great Chicago politico, said that "all politics is local." Some say that someday all law will be international. As trade barriers and immigration strictures fall and the world becomes interconnected by computer wires, family ties, and MTV, more and more lawyers will have to acquaint themselves with international issues.

Every day sophisticated corporate and other business transactions, or the businesses themselves, cross national boundaries. International lawyers know the ins and outs of dealing with different governments that could block these transnational transactions.

Governments are more interested in stimulating than smothering investment these days, however. One of the hottest areas for lawyers in 1995 was in the burgeoning field of "project finance," a corporate specialty involving raising capital for major new industrial or construction undertakings. And one of the hottest spots in this hot area is international, as emerging markets in Asia and elsewhere undertake huge new infrastructure projects.

There's also international litigation, which can mean representing a client from home in a foreign court or being involved in litigation that takes place in international forums such as the World Court. Usually, again, specialists in international litigation reside within the litigation departments of firms in major cities with international ties, such as New York, Los Angeles, San Francisco, and Miami.

LABOR LAW

Labor lawyers are another variety of litigator-corporate hybrid. They advise their business clients on the legality of hiring and firing practices, the law regarding fair labor standards, regulation of the work environment, and negotiations with unions. Union counsel do more or less the same thing, only they give the advice to unions and typically (though not always) make less money doing it. Sometimes labor lawyers represent their clients before government arbitration or mediation boards, or in courts, where the worst labor disputes often end up.

ERISA

Another sub-specialty for labor lawyers is understanding the law surrounding pension plans, which is regulated by a set of federal laws called ERISA (Employee Retirement Income Security Act). ERISA lawyers advise their clients regarding how pensions can be funded, when they "vest" (become a worker's right), how they are administered, and how they may be terminated.

If it sounds a little like tax law, that's because it is a little like tax law. But considering that employee pension funds are among the most powerful institutional investors in the country, there's clearly more going on in pensions than you might have thought.

Her Name Was ERISA. . .

Al Erreich laughs when asked if he'd wanted to be an ERISA lawyer as the gleam in his eyes foretold a successful career in the law. "Yeah," he says, "Ever since I was a young child."

Erreich's primary interest actually was tax work. But as a summer associate at the white-shoe Manhattan firm of Dewey Ballantine, the 1988 Columbia graduate was exposed to ERISA for the first time. "ERISA is kind of a cousin, or maybe a step-sister, of tax," he says. "I liked that it was relatively self-contained. It seemed possible to really know the topic, as opposed to a general tax lawyer who can never really grasp the whole tax code."

Now he doubts that even all of ERISA can be "mastered," but he's glad he made the decision to stick with it. After leaving Dewey for a stint in the legal department of accounting firm Ernst & Young, he settled in at New York's Roberts & Holland, a thirty-five-lawyer tax boutique. Besides his straight ERISA work, like most ERISA lawyers he also advises clients on tax issues surrounding executive compensation.

"Tax is more driven by mergers and acquisitions," he says. When the transactions dry up, corporate tax people are idle. "ERISA is influenced by M&A, so we're always in demand," he explains.

REAL ESTATE

Real estate lawyers are corporate lawyers, though in some larger firms they are set off in their own department. Just as corporate lawyers work on business transactions, real estate lawyers deal with transactions involving buying, selling, or leasing real property (real estate).

Real property isn't the opposite of unreal property. It's any property that isn't personal property. Mostly, real estate is land, or more generally "space," such as a unit in a high-rise building. (Technically, some very large things, such as buildings themselves, can be real property; it depends on if they're more or less permanently attached to the ground.)

One of the consistent aspects of real estate practice is that it involves financing. Virtually no real estate changes hand in this country without a mortgage being involved. A mortgage, of course, is a contract. Money is lent to the buyer, which the buyer promises to return by signing a "note," also called a "promissory note." The buyer also signs a mortgage. In the mortgage, she promises to give the property to the lender if she doesn't pay the lender back. Thus a mortgage is a specialized kind of security interest, i.e., the property is "security" for the loan.

Real estate lawyers work on the specific terms for financing real estate deals, which can often get quite complicated. They also ensure that the property being sold has "clear title," i.e., that the seller really owns it, and no one else can make a claim on it. And if there are zoning, environmental, or other regulatory hurdles to a proposed use of the land, clients turn to their real estate lawyers to represent them, sometimes in quasi-litigation contexts (such as before a zoning board or similar body).

BANKRUPTCY

Congress's authority to establish bankruptcy laws is set out in the Constitution. The bankruptcy system enables people and businesses who are in over their heads to get a "fresh start" while minimizing the damage done to creditors. In terms of the substantive law, you have to learn to be a bankruptcy lawyer; the practice is more like tax than anything else. But it plays like corporate or litigation when in action.

Bankruptcy is the boom specialty that fizzled. When the real-estate boom of the 1980s ended, bankruptcy looked like the place to be, and for a while it was. Bankruptcy specialists sprung their clients' bankruptcy filings on the world in the early dawn, while creditors slept. Then they litigated over the shape of the plan: how many cents on the dollar different "classes" of creditors would each get, how the reorganized company would look, whether current management would be allowed to remain in charge.

But soon players started observing how interminable the bankruptcy process was. Some "reorganizations" stretched out over years and years. The only people who really made out in the process were (here it comes) bankruptcy lawyers.

Now when businesses get in too deep, they merely use the *threat* of bankruptcy to encourage their creditors to sit down and work something out. In some cases a bankruptcy court is called in at the end to give its blessing to the plan. This is called a "pre-packaged bankruptcy." Lawyers are still needed for these workouts, but they're corporate lawyers; the bankruptcy crew just sweeps up the mess.

Nonetheless, there will always be a bankruptcy bar. Some things can't be worked out. And consumer bankruptcy won't go away; creditors are less likely to come to a global settlement with you and me than they are with K-Mart. On the other side of the table, lawyers who represent creditors (the "creditors' rights" bar) will always have mortgage foreclosures (taking over property when mortgage payments aren't made) and similar secured-assets work to do.

HEALTH LAW

As America ages and medical technology gets better and more expensive, the healthcare sector swells as a sector of the national economy. How far behind can healthcare lawyers be?

Healthcare lawyers work on a gamut of issues, mostly in a corporate mode. They are involved with owners and operators of healthcare facilities, such as hospitals, nursing homes, and clinics. These institutions need guidance on dealing with the an array of federal and state regulations in their fields, as well as the financing of their endeavors and the wide world of insurance.

On the more exotic end, healthcare lawyers are asked to provide guidance on tricky issues such as long-term care of the elderly, AIDS research, providers' legal and ethical obligations to their patients, experimental drugs, euthanasia, and managed care. Some attorneys actually specialize in medical ethics.

ENVIRONMENTAL LAW

In the last century and a quarter we Americans have dug up, built, and spat out a lot of junk. Unfortunately, we didn't do such a great job cleaning up after ourselves. From this, a very lucrative legal specialty was born.

Over the last twenty years or so, Congress and the states have passed far-ranging environmental protection laws. Besides mandating stricter controls for dumping than ever existed before, it imposed retroactive responsibility on polluters by instituting a simple three-part test for liability that is quite clear: (1) Did you own the property? (2) Did it become polluted while you owned it? (3) Where's your money? Some of these clean-up efforts cost tens, some hundreds of millions of dollars. This can stretch the resources of most companies. (See "Bankruptcy.") It also makes for lots of lawyers getting into the action between property owners, de facto polluters, government agencies, adjacent property owners, and insurance companies to see who'll end up holding the bag.

Lawyers Abhor a Vacuum

It's a bit of an exaggeration to say that the best thing to happen to the only attorney in town is when another one moves in. But legal specialties do tend to spin off legal specialties. Indeed, there are lawyers who specialize in suing other lawyers for malpractice. They don't get too many invitations to the Hamptons.

One such spin-off specialty is the plaintiff's insurance-coverage litigation bar. These are the ones who sue insurance companies that, hiding behind their lawyers' interpretations of insurance policies, deny that the person or company that bought the insurance was insured for the kind of claim being made.

This is a common problem in the field of environmental litigation, since insurance companies are anxious not to be stuck with massive liability for risks no one foresaw ten, twenty, or thirty years ago. Covered parties who are successful in these suits often recover punitive or multiple damages, awarded as a counter-incentive for that very behavior. Their lawyers often work on some variation of a contingency fee.

ENTERTAINMENT AND SPORTS LAW

Some of us never grow up. The adolescents among us who become doctors want to be sports doctors, and the adolescents among us who become lawyers want to be sports (and entertainment) lawyers. Actually, almost *everyone* wants to be a sports or entertainment lawyer.

These lawyers represent their clients in corporate and other business transactions, sometimes even advising their clients as agents in the negotiation of contracts. They are usually people with skills that propel them to the top of their fields. Stars don't have to settle for less and may be prone to a bit more temperament than the typical CEO. They usually have a lot of money on the table.

To make it into glam-law, you have to be a very, very good lawyer. And knowledge of the industry in which you'd like to work is, of course, a prerequisite. Charm won't hurt you at all. But for most people, getting to be a lawyer to the stars requires, as much as anything else, contacts, or at least the kind of savvy and dint for self-promotion that can get them for you.

CHAPTER SIX

Resourceful You

Now that you're on track and have wrestled with those existential going-to-law school demons, it's time to check out the status of some less metaphysical resources: time and money. Neither of these is to be taken for granted, and, with all due respect, few people just cracking their 20s really have a grip on either one, much less how to evaluate them in terms of legal education.

TIME

The question isn't whether you have time for law school in between "Seinfeld" reruns, your four-hour-a-day workout, and an all-important social life. This book doesn't address the management of your time while in law school. Rather, the question is whether you have three years (full time) or more (part time) to devote to the study of law in the scheme of your life.

For people planning to go to law school right after graduation (see chapter 8), the difference between starting "real life" at 22 or at 25 is small. The significance of the respective years seems to increase as time goes on, though. It's one thing to decide to start a new career when you're 35. But it's another to realize that, by the time you prepare for and take the LSATs, apply and get accepted, attend and finish law school, and get a job, you could be feeling the hot breath of 40 on your neck.

THE CHILDREN'S HOUR

People with obligations in their lives other than to themselves have to take the time commitment of law school and law practice more seriously. It goes without saying that it would be difficult to run a bakery and attend law school at the same time (giving up lost income and business opportunities are discussed later in this chapter). There are other obligations, however, to consider when evaluating if you have time for law school. Family obligations may look easier to push aside than economic ones. But unlike monetary sacrifice, the sacrifice of family time and involvement is well-nigh impossible to replace.

Being a spouse or parent requires the investment of time. Time spent on law school, instead of with the important people in your life, may pay off in the long run, of course, because your professional success may enable you later in life to devote more time to them. As anyone who's read the previous chapters should be able to tell you, the chances of this are slim since successful lawyers are extremely busy people.

On the other hand, having more secure prospects for income may be the kind of payoff that makes the sacrifice of "family time" worthwhile. Almost everyone has to be prepared to make sacrifices to support his or her family. If it's possible to stay afloat while attending law school, sacrificing time may well be worth it. Lawyers, again, are among the highest paid professionals. If your talent and credentials are such that you've got a realistic chance of joining in the bounty, you may be able to provide for your family in a way that will pay off for generations.

Remember, though, that law school is a sacrifice of time, one of many, many sacrifices you will make as you embark on a career in law. Whether you're married and have children today, or will in the future, be prepared to write off more than the typical amount of time with your spouse and kids.

Because the Night

One way to cheat the challenges, temporal and economic (see below), of attending law school is to get your degree in a part-time program that stretches out over four or more years instead of three. Night school was good enough for Fiorella LaGuardia, the great reform mayor of New York, who graduated from New York University's night law school program around the turn of the century. It also did well by the late Chief Justice Warren Burger, who graduated from the night law program at William Mitchell College of Law (now St. Paul College of Law) in 1931.

The early night law school programs catered to second-generation immigrants like LaGuardia who were anxious to get on the American merry-go-round of success. There was some initial resistance to night law schools from the established law schools (mostly those affiliated with major universities), but eventually both the ABA and the AALS (the American Association of Law Schools) worked with these programs to bring their academic standards up to those of full-time institutions. Accreditation standards, including the devotion of faculty and other resources to student needs, are the same for both full- and part-time students.

Nonetheless, the perception of night school studies, and night school students, as "something less" survives. Indeed, when NYU's star began to rise on the national law school scene in the late 1970s and early 1980s, the night school was jettisoned to ensure the school's unencumbered ascent. (It worked.)

In reality, studies have shown that night-school students at schools that also have day divisions are a lot like the day crowd. The main difference in such schools is that, the more modest the school, the better the night school students look next to the full-timers. But for both sets of students, placement and career paths have more to do with class rank than in which division the student is.

Night students do tend to be older (five to six years) and poorer than day students. This shouldn't surprise you, since generally the main reason for attending law school at night is that the student can't afford to give up her day job. (As a corollary, some companies, such as engineering and technology firms and some legal publishers, will pay for an employee's night law school, but this is much rarer than with business school.) For much the same reason, all agree that such students are usually more mature and better motivated than their full-time peers.

Nonetheless, people attending night school are attempting to burn the candle at both ends. Something has to give, and all the motivation in the world won't make up for the stress, the exhaustion, and the conflicting schedules that come with part-time attendance. Thus, night school students tend to have lower GPAs, and, though data is scanty, some published reports have claimed that they have attenuated career opportunities, which is concomitant with lower performance.

Do employers, looking at identical records of night and evening students, discriminate between them? The evidence is mostly anecdotal. Some are impressed with the gumption and work ethic of a night student who perseveres and achieves. Others are prejudiced against part-timers because they're typically older (see chapter 8). They may also believe either that night students are less committed to the profession because they haven't made law school a full-time proposition or that they've had to endure less rigorous competition and evaluation.

Everyone involved in night law school agrees on one thing: It's hard fighting a battle on two or more fronts. Most part-time programs involve taking at least one course during the summer. And, of course, working as a law clerk or summer associate is most likely out of the question.

But for some, part-time study is the only chance they have at making a dream come true. For the right person, at the right time, with the right background, a law degree after five years could make all the difference. After all, it did for LaGuardia and Burger.

OPPORTUNITY COSTS

Nothing's free. Even opportunity has a cost, and that cost is what economists call "opportunity cost." Opportunity cost is the price you pay when, by doing something, you forego the opportunity to do something else. Using a basic example, the time you spend attending law school represents (in addition to its financial costs discussed below) a sacrifice of time that may have been spent flipping dino-burgers at $5.43 an hour or doing brain surgery at $150 a minute. Opportunity cost also includes the non-financial gain that you give up by choosing to do something like going to a concert, hanging out with friends, dating, going to the movies with your spouse, or reading a bedtime story to your kids. Here, however, the focus is on opportunity cost of a dollars-and-cents kind.

The fundamental question in evaluating opportunity cost is, how much do you stand to benefit to incur that cost? Someone who's making $150,000 a year as a business executive will have a hard time justifying (economically) the loss of $450,000 in income over three years, not including bonuses and increases, to attend law school. Even under the best case scenario, only a very small percentage of those coming out of law school make more than $85,000.

That's the short-term analysis. It is possible to be in a dead-end $150,000 job, or perhaps it's in an industry that itself is doomed. If the same executive ends up, fifteen years from now, one of the lucky few to be admitted to a law partnership where per-partner profits may be $200,000, $500,000 or more, that $450,000 opportunity cost may be forgotten quickly.

At the other extreme, someone making $25,000 would be giving up approximately $75,000 in income by attending law school. He could make that $75,000 or more in one year upon graduation though that amount would be about double the typical law graduate's salary. Still, people in college with little prospect for gainful, career-oriented employment get automatic credit here; their financial opportunity cost is so low as to not be a factor.

All this focus on financial opportunity costs (see next section for "cost costs") is not to obscure the fact that you may decide to make what seems like a lousy economic deal for perfectly good reason. The executive making $150,000 may be miserable running the widget factory and may reasonably conclude that a career as a public defender would make his spirit soar. Whatever. As long as he knows the costs, both obvious and hidden, his decision to enroll in law school can be made intelligently.

PAYING THE PIPER

Attending law school is getting more expensive. While inflation across the economy has stabilized in the last decade or so to under 5 percent, law school tuition gallops like Carter-era gasoline.

If you took basic economics, you'll remember something called "demand pull" inflation, where "too many" dollars chase after "too few" widgets, driving up the price. That's exactly what happened when the oil supply was artificially reduced in the 1970s. (The other kind is "cost-push" inflation, which happens when it gets more expensive to supply something.)

From the mid-1980s until the early 1990s, the demand for places in law school increased markedly. There was some increase in supply—more law schools, bigger law school classes—but it didn't keep up with demand. That gets you an increase in price, especially, as here, where there are few easy substitutes.

The Sellers' Market

At the "top ten" schools in the country (we'll spare you the list), whose seats are among the most in demand by applicants, tuition increased an average of 75 percent from 1986 through 1992—a period during which the Consumer Price Index (CPI) went up less than 30 percent. Overall, the Bureau of Labor Statistics reports that, during roughly the same period, law school tuition rose 66 percent.

One disconcerting fact is that the increase in tuition has been led by public institutions, notably top state schools that are among the national elite. In an era of budget-cutting, legislatures have figured out that there's little reason for the people of a state to subsidize the legal education of people from other states. The Universities of Michigan and Virginia now charge fees that differ little from their Ivy League counterparts (around $17,000 a year) to out-of-state residents; both have doubled their tuition since 1986. And while other top state schools, such as the University of Texas and the University of California at Berkeley haven't reached that level, they have increased their non-resident tuitions by even larger percentages—more than triple for Texas.

The overall increase in law school tuition may slow, for by all reports the number of applications to law school is at least leveling off. (Applications in 1995 were actually somewhat higher than in previous years, which had shown a decline.) Some of the larger, less in-demand schools have actually starting reducing class sizes to "keep quality up," though the medium-run effect is to keep tuition, per student, up as well. The combination of more realism about the prospects for economic success in the legal profession and the simple shrinking of the college-graduate age group should cause this trend to continue. But for the schools that remain in demand, with four, five, or in the case of Yale, fourteen applicants for every seat, these demographic changes will never affect tuition trends.

Your Uncle Sam

One of the ironies about the generosity of government sponsored financial aid programs is that it has contributed to the demand side of demand-pull inflation. In other words, it has made law school more expensive by adding to the number of available dollars out there chasing those J.D.s. Now tuition of all kinds is so expensive that affording it is unimaginable without loans for almost everyone. Government, then, is solidly in the business of supporting law and other schools of higher education, private or otherwise.

All of which makes law schooling a nice business to be in. Once a school has its library, some classrooms, and all that other stuff the ABA and the AALS ask a school to have, there's a minimum of cash needed to keep the thing running. The main expense, besides maintaining the bricks and mortar, is faculty salaries; an expense, as mentioned earlier, that may very well be going down at some schools. On the other hand, if you can get six, seven, or twelve hundred people to shell out an average of $10,000 a year (allowing for scholarships), that comes to 6, 7, 12 million dollars a year in income for your favorite tax-free, non-profit educational institution.

THE WHOLE CHECK:
THE ECONOMICS OF TUITION PRICING

The cost of attending law school, including the cost of living (no matter what you think, you do have to pay to live), ranges from as little at $30,000 at a public institution in a place with a low cost of living, to over $100,000 at a private school in an expensive city. Both numbers are pretty big, though there's also a big difference between them.

A median figure, however, would be worse than misleading, because tuition amounts are something of a fiction. Most institutions such as colleges and law schools engage extensively in what economists call "cross-subsidization." Those with more money subsidize, or contribute to, the education of those with less money through the financial-aid system. People who can afford the full price, or who, under the financial-aid formulas (see below) can "afford" to borrow the full price, are charged more than the price basic supply and demand would dictate to make up for the reduced tuition charged to the needier students.*

What this amounts to is that, notwithstanding the "sticker price," the actual price of law school after cross-subsidization depends a great deal on how much financial aid money is available to the school, how little it can afford to charge needy students, and how many needy students it decides to admit. All this goes into the formula

---

* In fact, this could be perfect "price discrimination," which makes sellers happy since they get every last penny a person would be willing to spend on something before deciding it's too much. The system doesn't go this far because the posted tuition price is a cap, or maximum price. Thus the super rich pay no more than the rich.

that's applied when evaluating the individual's own financial situation, if she applies for aid. Thus, although some of the best-known names in legal education post the highest tuition and fees (around $20,000 a year), they may end up cheaper than many a bargain brand, because of the financial-aid resources available to the wealthy, established institutions.

How do you get a piece of these "financial aid resources"? The financial aid system is based on a mix, to be discussed below, of "contributions" (your money), scholarship (the school's money), and loans (a bank's money). There may be political support for a theoretical "right" to attend college. But that "right" hasn't made it to law school, and there's very little "free money" out there, besides what better-off law schools can kick in.

Law school can be a kind of vortex. The kind of people who apply to law school are often those who start applying for things before really understanding if they want them. This applies to applying and qualifying for financial aid. It is a good idea to really understand what kind of debt, and what kind of terms, attending law school portends *before* starting those gears turning on how to get some. This is a serious business that many 1980s law students are only beginning to comprehend. Thus, an "eyes on the prize" exercise is advised.

SOMETHING BORROWED

Since few people have several tens of thousands of dollars on hand, most folks have to borrow money to pay for law school and for their living expenses. You may well ask who would lend a callow, unemployed person such as yourself such sums? The answer: They're lining up for the privilege.

There are several reasons these cascades of money are available to you. One is that lenders have seen those NALP statistics quoted at the beginning of the book. Most lawyers are good credit risks, and indeed few are willing to face the ignominy of bankruptcy. (Don't get any smart ideas. These loans aren't dischargeable by bankruptcy for ten years.)

The other reason is that these loans are made by the government. They used to be merely insured or guaranteed by the government. Banks basically got to make a little profit for handling the origination and paperwork of lending this money before they turned around and sold the loans off to big clearinghouses. Now, under the William D. Ford Federal Direct Loan program, the banks have been taken out of the process completely.

There are several categories of official loans, many of them named after the congresspersons who thought them up. The financial aid atmosphere is thick with names like Perkins, Stafford, and the like. The problem is that some of these loans are being phased out under the Ford program and some aren't; this is currently a topic of wrangling between those famously cooperative types on Capitol Hill and Pennsylvania Avenue. To complicate matters, some schools are "participants" in the Ford program, and others aren't.

Thus your best source of information will remain the most up-to-date materials published by the Law Services organization of the Law School Admissions Council (the LSAT people) and the financial aid information made available by the specific school. Nonetheless, for purposes of providing perspective, these are the broad outlines of the kind of numbers you, as a law student and law school graduate, may be juggling into the next century. Unless otherwise noted, payment and accrual of interest does not begin until graduation, with an available grace period of six to nine months. Most give you ten or as many as fifteen years to pay the money back.

- **The Perkins Loan,** once called the National Direct Student Loan, is still the best deal going. As the old name implies, it's money that is lent directly to students by the government. Its 5 percent annual interest rate means that its "real" interest rate (the amount of interest above the inflation rate) is virtually zero. Needy (discussed below) students may qualify for up $5,000 a year to a maximum of $30,000 in Perkins debt (including undergrad debt). Schools get Perkins money in blocks and decide for themselves how to spend it; thus, a big or poor school may max out at $1,000 per head; basically, your books budget plus student activities fees and some chips.

- **The Stafford Loan** is the renamed Guaranteed Student Loan (GSL), as older students will know it. During the Reagan era, the government decided it was a little too guaranteed; some utterly need-less students were borrowing thousands at the old 7 percent rate and buying

15 percent certificates of deposit with the money. They spoiled it for everyone. Now all applicants are need-tested, and rates are variable, with a 9 percent cap (though if you have old GSL debt you get to keep that rate forever, even on new Stafford funds). You could, as of the date of publication, borrow $8,000 a year of this stuff, up to a maximum GSL/Stafford cumulative amount of $65,000.

Note: In the event that you have a moment of good feeling about this money being available to you, it can be tempered by the realization that while you may qualify and indebt yourself for some amount of Stafford debt, an "origination fee" of up to 5 percent and an "insurance premium" of up to 3 percent will be taken right off the top. Thus you will sign a note for, say, $5,000, but only 92 percent of that ($4,600) will be disbursed to your school. You owe the whole five grand, but as far as the school's concerned, you've come up with the $4,600. Welcome to the real world.

- **Supplemental Student Loan (SLS)** is the loan that gets you over the hump: The difference between the amount that the financial-aid formula (discussed below) deems you and your family can afford to pay, and the amount you really can pay. This is practically a plain, old bank loan, not even need-based, only it's made possible by a government guarantee. Thus the latest information is that the SLS is lent out at the present Treasury Bill rate plus 3.25 percent, a nice little profit margin for the lender, considering that it's insured. Also, unlike other loans, SLS interest starts to run (and, depending on your lender, payments may be due) as soon as you borrow it. The SLS also may have a 3 percent insurance fee. You can have up to $20,000 of this, $4,000 at a time.

- **Law Access Loan (LAL)** is the financial-aid arm of Law Services. Its terms are like the SLS except that your real credit record will be checked. You can get up to $13,500 a year of LAL money, the largest annual loan available, up to a lifetime max of $120,000, or $150,000 with a cosigner. The Law Access program has a form that enables you to apply for the Stafford and SLS loans at the same time as the LAL, which you'll have to do anyway to have a shot at LAL money.

More Help

The Law School Admissions Council (LSAC), mandarin of the LSAT and lord of the law school application process, has the most up-to-date financial aid information. You can get the LSAC's book, Financial Aid for Law School: A Preliminary Guide, by calling (215) 968-1001.

A LIFE IN CHAINS

Law school graduates have a tendency to get glassy eyed over their law school debt, but there is something stunning about being an unemployed 25-year-old who owes $75,000 and can't live on what that money bought. There was a time not so long ago when the interest on these loans was, like all interest, tax deductible. Since these loans are often amortized in the same way as mortgages (you start out paying all interest, and you slowly pay more and more on the principal until your last payment is all principal) you could deduct virtually the whole cost of your early years of loan repayments from your income. No more. And to people who borrowed under those circumstances? Tough.

What must be understood, therefore, is that there is no magic to this debt. It is not somehow different from any other debt, except, as mentioned earlier, it is harder to get out of by declaring bankruptcy. It is real money, really owed to real creditors who will really hound you or sue you if you fall behind.

You want numbers? Someone with a $68,000 loan burden has to pay $800 a month to lenders. That equals $9,600 a year. A "mere" $500 a month payment adds up to $6,000 a year. Thus the typical law graduate's $37,000 annual salary is chopped down to $27,400, or $31,000 before taxes. Even someone making $85,000 in a big New York firm will feel $800 a month; her $85,000 becomes $75,400; after taxes, maybe she's taking home $50,000. A nice income? Not too shabby. Just don't confuse it with wealth.

SOME KIND OF WAY OUT OF HERE

Are there alternatives to these hefty monthly payments? There are a couple, but, short of marrying into money, there's little you can do to avoid the necessity of remunerating providers of midday comestibles (there's no free lunch). Here are some ways you can at least avoid some indigestion.

Loan Refinancing

You can refinance your loan, with its onerous ten- or fifteen-year payback schedules, to a more leisurely twenty- or twenty-five year repayment schedule. Sallie Mae, the alias of SLMA, the Student Loan Marketing Association (the servicing agency that, in various guises, buys most student loans from commercial lenders), offers a program called "Smart Loan." (Some other sources offer these programs, though none do as much as SLMA.) Smart Loan enables you to combine all your student loans except LALs into one big loan with a blended interest rate and a longer repayment period.

Borrowers who owe at least $7,500 can reduce their monthly payments, at least up front (depending on the program selected), by 40 percent. Here are some for-instances, which will depend on prevalent interest rates and how much of which loan you have:

Debt amount			
$9,000	$13,000	$25,000	$50,000
Original monthly payment			
$116	$170	$328	$667
Refinanced monthly payment			
$68	$98	$188	$375

So what's the catch? One of the basic principles of finance is that the cost of a loan is decided by the interest rate and the amount of time the money is borrowed for. In other words, if you consolidate your loans, you'll end up paying more interest over all; if it's a lot of debt, and if your rate happens to be high, *tens of thousands more*. You're welcome, of course, to apply cost-discounting to this amount; i.e., to figure out the value of a dollar in the year 2020 in terms of today's money. This will make you feel a little better, since even at the present rate of modest inflation, $800 a month will seem a lot less dramatic when you're in your fifties.

But are you prepared to keep making payments into your fifties? And if you apply our opportunity-cost principles and ask what else you might want to do with $800 a month for all those years besides pay for the law degree you're considering today, it all comes out kind of depressing.

The Last Deduction

When Congress took away the deduction for interest expenses, it left one kind of interest-expense deduction in place: Interest on home mortgages. So if you or your parents have a home with equity in it, you or they can borrow against it. Besides getting a better rate than anything but a Perkins, the homeowner will be able to deduct the interest from income.

The problems with this can be seen in two categories: the obvious and the less obvious. The obvious include the fact that most people who want to go to law school don't have homes. If their parents do, this scheme works fine as long as it's the parents paying the loan back. A homeowner can't use her home-interest deduction to write off interest paid by someone else—the idea isn't to put homeowners in the lending business. The IRS does not appreciate sham home-mortgage loans that are just a cover up for one person using someone else's home-mortgage deduction. Although, as discussed below, financial-aid authorities see the matter differently, the IRS doesn't care if you're all family. If you don't have a legal interest in the property, you can't use the deduction.

Less obvious problems spring from the fact that a home mortgage deduction comes with a home mortgage. The borrower is putting the house up as security for the loan, meaning that if there's a default, the house goes to the lender. This isn't the case with student loans. Defaulting on them means, ultimately, that a court issues a judgment, which results in an order of execution, but one that is satisfied by every means possible short of taking someone's real property.

Also, all student loan programs allow for deferments and grace periods when there is a loss of income or other serious event. Home mortgages don't.

THE FORMULA

So how is financial aid eligibility—the right to, at best, tuition reduction, and, for the rest, the privilege to borrow money a bit cheaper—determined? It's based on the information you will provide on the uniform Free Application for Federal Student Aid form, or FAFSA, and possibly a supplemental form used by your school or another uniform form called the Financial Aid Profile. The data on these forms is fed into the maw of the formula with the depressing moniker of "the Congressional Methodology" or the "Federal Methodology."

The idea of the Congressional Methodology is to figure out a number called the Expected Family Contribution, or EFC. The EFC is the sum of the Student Contribution and the Parent Contribution. The system analyzes your assets, liabilities, and income to determine how much you can afford to pay for law school. Ideally, this number, plus the amount of financial aid made available to you, will equal or at least come close to the school's "budget," also called the "Cost of Attendance" (COA). This includes tuition, living expenses, fees, books, travel to and from school, and even some allowance for personal expenses. The government's formula for the Expected Student Contribution is based on half of a student's summer earnings above $1,750 and 35 percent of her reported assets.

Having said that, your law school is free to ignore any or all of these criteria in making its award of its resources, i.e., tuition reduction (grants) or school-scholarship loans. Individual schools apply their own methodology and may look at subjective factors, or the "big picture," in deciding your award. Though individual schools may have different formulas, the general rule is that a student can expect to see a third of his assets and half of his previous summer's income deemed available for his contribution.

Graduate students are automatically considered "independent" by the government, for purposes of authorizing federal financial aid (which, for law students, means loans). Schools will look at your parents' assets, both earned and unearned income, the age of the older parent, the size of your family and how many family members are or will be enrolled in higher education, even the amount of equity in their home (which the government is not allowed to consider, even for dependent students), though not money already in an IRA, 401K, Keogh, or other retirement plans.

What if your parents say, "You're on your own," with regard to law school? Your school will invite you to take out the shortfall in SLS or LAL loans. But cheer up. By the time you have kids in college and law school, you could still be paying these loans off, which can only have a good impact on your kids' award packages.

CHAPTER SEVEN

The Shortest, Gladdest Years of Your Life

You've determined that you have the talent, the commitment, the understanding, and the resources for law school. Now comes the fun part: preparing for law school and getting into one you want to attend. Your time in college is central to both preparing for and getting into law school.

In terms of preparation, if you're even remotely law school material you've come a long way academically from your high school days. College is grownup learning, more self-directed and self-motivated than most people experience in high school. And by the end of college, you should, by virtue of your bachelor's degree, have developed not an expertise, but a good understanding of at least one subject area. This process can be more or less useful in your law school preparation. Even if you're in the fall semester of senior year you may be able to improve your first-year experiences in law school through your course selection for the spring semester.

When it comes to getting into the law school of your choice, neither board scores, activities, lifelong ambitions, nor money comes close in importance to your undergraduate career, i.e., your grades. (This is less true for older students, as will be discussed in the next chapter.) When a law school is trying to determine how you handle academic work, what could be of more value than your transcript?

UNDERGRAD ARCHITECTURE

Some prelaw students make the mistake of thinking of college as a lobby for their expected entry through the portals of law school. There's no question that you can take this approach, and perhaps even succeed with it; at least if you define success as getting into a "good" law school.

But this approach is an unfortunate one, because college is not a waiting room for law school; it's an educational foundation, ideally for your entire life. With this in mind, it's best not to have law school tunnel vision in selecting your courses and your major, depriving you of what is almost certain to be your last chance to get the benefits that college is meant to impart.

You should think of college as something you build on. If you build a legal career on it, that's great. But if the legal career doesn't work out, your undergraduate foundation can be used for any kind of edifice. Whereas if you merely build an anteroom to a legal career, you risk constructing nothing but an expensive, time-wasting, and unsightly hallway to nowhere.

For that reason, though this book is called The Prelaw Companion, you should banish the p-word from your vocabulary—at least as a noun. Thus, a course may be "a good prelaw course," but don't be "a prelaw" or let yourself be described as "studying prelaw."

Certainly never choose a major called "prelaw," which is offered at some colleges. (Obviously, if there's still time, don't choose a college based on whether it offers this major!) Besides being a generally bogus concept, it will certainly leave you at the bottom of an abyss if you realize, either after finishing this book or in May of your senior year, that you were born to dance or pursue some other unlawyerly path. If you're just positive you're "a prelaw," you can accomplish the same thing as you would with this so-called major by taking traditional courses like politics, government, history, and economics. But avoid attaching such a loserly label like "prelaw" to your transcript.

This advice doesn't only apply to the so-called prelaw major. Regardless of your major, be a college student who wants to get the most out of his undergraduate experience and who is considering law school as a step in the future. By doing so you'll be the best "prelaw" you can be.

"Let me handle it, I'm prelaw..."

... says the gung-ho member of Delta House, the Animal House fraternity being pilloried in the "Pan-Hellenic Council" of "Faber College" in National Lampoon's early 1980's hit, Animal House. "I thought you were premed," says a fellow Delta brother. "Same thing," replies the young Daniel Webster . . .

The joke is on everyone who thinks being a prelaw is like being a premed. Really, "prelaw" is the bastard cousin of premed. Pre-medical school students have a specific cycle of courses they have to take during their four years to even qualify to apply to medical school. Along with excelling in these courses, they have to ace practically everything they touch in college in order to make it through the extraordinarily competitive medical school admissions system.

But the only prelaw requirement is a bachelor's degree. Though this chapter discusses certain types of courses that someone thinking of law school would do well to consider taking, many successful legal careers have been built without them. Frankly, regardless of what you think of doctors, someone who's a premed and stays that way has really accomplished something. Whereas being a prelaw is just a ticket to Dweebesville. Don't buy it. Be a mensch who might go to law school, not a prelaw.

In this section, the discussion is about different majors. The point to keep in mind is that courses in all these topics may be useful subjects to learn without a multiyear commitment to concentrating in them, a point that will be revisited below.

The Argument for the Prelaw Major

There are certain major courses of study that are always regarded as "well suited" to law school study. As mentioned above, they are government, political science, history, and, to a somewhat lesser extent, economics and undergraduate business. People who want to go to law school have always flocked to these majors. The main reason is, not surprisingly, the subject matter of the material studies in these different fields, which are discussed in more depth later in this chapter:

- **Government**, obviously, is to some extent about law, and its students spend much of their time discussing purposeful aggregations of law, which is one definition of "policy." There is probably no better preparation for law school, if by preparation one means covering similar subject matter, than a government or public-policy major.

- **Political science** is related to government, but is somewhat more abstract and often deals with the interactions between governments. (Thus it is the "macro" to the government major's "micro.")

- **History** can bring excellent perspective to legal study and can assist one in understanding the development of legal doctrine over time. In this regard, American history is especially valuable.

- **Economics**, probably the least popular of these four among prelaw students, may be abstract, but much of it deals with the making of policy.

- **Business** majors, such as general business, accounting, finance, and marketing, are usually people who want a "practical" major, and to this extent they are the same kind of people who go to law school. The subject matter taught in these majors is useful in more advanced law school courses but has virtually no bearing on the all-important first year of law school.

In the Beginning Was the Word

Besides the substantive usefulness of these majors, they are popular among people considering law school because, with the exception of economics, they're verbal majors, which is another way of saying they're not quantitative.

You'll notice that in earlier chapters, quantitative skill (as opposed to general analytical ability) is not mentioned as critical for most lawyers. It isn't. Thus, many people who have math anxiety, but who want to be "professionals," look at the professional smorgasbord of medical school, business school, law school and see only one dish that doesn't require math.

As for economics (and, to a lesser extent, undergraduate business, and accounting) the folks who take these are not the math scaredycats. Indeed, they're often weighing the law-school-versus-business-school (or even medical school) question right up to the end.

Either way, to the extent that any of these courses of study encourage one to read and write on an advanced level, as discussed later, a person considering law school will benefit.

A Major Concession

So what about history, government, and political science majors? The considerations that make them so popular are legitimate. It may make sense for you to choose one of these as your focus if you want to go to law school because of the substantive advantages laid out above. But be aware of a couple of traps:

- **Groupthink**—These majors are positively packed with "prelaws." If you're someone who can swim against the tide, then power to you; study what you want. But if you, like most people, are highly susceptible to group influence, any doubts you entertain about law school will be washed away in this crowd.

- **The conveyer belt**—Even if you're not so easily affected by the crowd, these majors tend to be "feeders" into law school. That is, very few people have thought out what else they can "do" with a political science major. That's true of a music major, too, but someone who majors in music probably doesn't have to worry about his path taking three years of his time and $80,000 in (probably borrowed) cash.

- **Admissions office boredom**—One thing that isn't going to perk up attention in your dream school's admissions office is another application from a politics major. But a behavioral biologist who wants to go to law school? Hey, that's kind of interesting . . .

What I Did for Love

As you may deduce from the last couple of paragraphs, there is a school of thought (favored by the author) that choosing a major based on a youthful infatuation with the idea of law school is a bad idea.

The ideal result of the "foundation" approach to undergraduate preparation for law school is that your college years be well-rounded and that you do what you like, or even love, as an undergraduate. This way, your foundation will be solid all the way around and will have the deep strength necessary for even the loftiest structure, including a legal career.

For Sentimental Reasons

There's also kind of a sentimental reason to be well-rounded academically: You are entering a learned profession. The American legal education system is unique in that you may not take full part in it until you have achieved a bachelor's degree in a subject besides law. The presumption, beyond the scope of this book to examine, is that you should be an educated person before you even begin to learn what a tort is. Such a person, theoretically, will be a better lawyer, a better counselor, and not least a better person. What a shame it would be to take the seven years of higher education needed to become a lawyer and turn them into seven years of legal education.

In terms of majors, according to this line of thought, you should do what you love, or at least like. Why?

- **You'll do well.** All but the most disciplined among us do much better at what we like. Doing well in college is the A-number-one factor for getting into the law school of your choice, and this reason is by far the best one to major in what you want.

- **Your options aren't closed.** Open any law school catalog and see if any of them require a certain major. They don't. You can always apply to and attend and even excel at law school, no matter what your undergrad background.

- **Your options are open.** If law school isn't in the cards, you may very well be able to follow up on your interest in basket weaving. Sound funny? See how much better you do following up on your interest in "policy."

- It can make you a good lawyer. Some people are able to combine an inherent interest in a non-legal field with their legal careers. True, these are among the luckiest people, but they're motivated, knowledgeable, and often connected. They could be you.

Some people like political science, of course, and they may be tickled about their major whether they end up in law school or the French Foreign Legion. But for those with a more lyrical bent, there is very little reason to recommend a "prelaw major."

Look: The Harvard Law School is full, terribly full, of majors in international affairs, political science, and all that jazz. But it's also got plenty of art majors, French majors, and even jazz majors. Most members of the former group had law school on the brain from some time around sophomore year. Members of the latter group worked hard also, but enjoyed their college experience, began to develop expertise in a topic they cared about, did well in their studies, and brought their personalities into fuller flower than they otherwise would have if they'd stuffed themselves into some grey "prelaw" box. Which group would you rather join?

It's Academic

There are other academic considerations in planning your undergraduate preparation for law school besides choosing your major.

Here's where we get a little more practical. Everything that was said earlier about "doing what you love," was said on the condition that no one take that too far. There are certain things you can accomplish as an undergraduate that will enhance your application and your preparation for law school. You should be able to demonstrate that:

- in applying for law school, you have at least an inkling as to what it may be about

- you didn't just take four years of gut classes and can handle rigorous material

- you have developed your analytical ability

- you have had sustained practice at writing

How can you achieve these undergraduate academic goals?

Perspective Electives: In the Big Four

One approach to improving your academic preparation for law school is to take courses in the fields mentioned above, even if you are a linguistics major. If some of these topics scare you or the thought of them bores you to tears, maybe they should be approached on a pass-fail or even audit basis. This is especially true for the non-quantitative areas, i.e., politics, government, and history.

Political science and government. Political science is probably the most popular prelaw major, especially since many fine under-graduate programs do not offer government or public policy under-graduate concentrations. The thing about political science, or "politics" as some schools call it, is that it's often a major in current events. It's the Chinese food of academia; a few years later, you're hungry again.

But political science does offer a person some savvy about what's going on in the world and in the country, which can bring depth to one's legal studies. For example, exposure to political science and government courses, especially at the introductory level, will do you some good as a preview of the kinds of topics that law school students spend a lot of time on. It's almost irresponsible to decide on a legal career without some insight into the world in which the legal profession operates. Lawyers are, by and large, men and women of affairs, at work within the civic machinery of our country. You ought to at least have a basic understanding of how that machinery works, which you may get in "100"-level courses with names like "The Democratic System." If your school offers a semi-official "prelaw course," such as constitutional interpretation, don't feel obligated to take it, but understand that it could be of some help.

Political science courses also frequently expose you to the el-ementary theoretical bases of democracy, government, and law. Courses that survey English and American political thought, such as the writings of John Locke, Roger Williams, the Federalists and their foes, William Lloyd Garrison, Abraham Lincoln, up through Woodrow Wilson, John Dewey, and Martin Luther King, Jr., are absolutely guaranteed to improve your comprehension of law school as well as your perfor-mance.

Finally, political science classes can shed light on the policy debates that will both underlie your first-year courses and be at the heart of more advanced law school classes such as family law, taxation, antitrust, and corporations. Exposure to the development of government social and economic activism that affect these and other crucial topics can enhance the legal part of your legal education, because you'll have the basics down already.

History. Courses in American history are useful for a similar reason. To some extent, this is a little like the "current events" major of poli-sci only without the "current" part. Thus the best reason to study history is that it adds perspective to legal study.

An example: No one can be expected to develop expertise from one or two undergraduate courses or even from majoring in a subject. But you have no right to take part in a law school class discussion on affirmative action or the Voting Rights Act if you don't know the basic story of slavery, the Civil War, Reconstruction, and the civil rights movement. You may have learned this in high school, but one college course in American social history or the like will bring your understanding up to a level appropriate for a professional.

Similarly, you'd be better off in that discussion if you knew about the contribution of Latinos and their ancestors to the exploration and settlement of this continent, and how the states of Texas, California, Florida, and virtually the whole Southwest went from being parts of Spanish or independent Mexico, to being states of the Union.

Economics and business. There really oughta be a law that you can't go to law school without taking at least one, and arguably two, economics courses—one in introductory microeconomics, one in introductory macroeconomics. Both are about the most straightforward way to learn what a "cost-benefit analysis" really is. "Micro" teaches a valuable way to model and attempt to predict behavior of atomic units such as people, companies, and families. This model is useful in every single law school course, and even if you don't buy it you have to understand it to battle those who do no matter what your legal specialty.

"Macro," which is about how these atomic actors work (or fail to work) in concert, is the bedrock of modern analysis in economic policy. If you're going to be a business lawyer, you should take this course as well as micro. But macro is arguably less broadly applicable than micro, so if you have to choose between the two, micro is the way to go.

Beyond the intro level, you don't really benefit in law school from the highly theoretical and abstract economic theory found even at the intermediate level, except in the general sense of honing your analytical powers. But courses in political economy, such as those addressing the distribution of income, the operation of the financial markets, and the international economy are obvious topics for people who see themselves practicing law in related areas.

Business. This brings us to the business curriculum, which at some schools is cleverly hidden in the economics department. There is probably little in this area that will have a direct effect on your basic skills and your first-year courses.

But there are some law school courses that virtually everyone takes, such as corporations, income tax, and commercial paper; such business-like courses can give you a great leg up. Moreover, anyone who sees herself on a track into a large law firm that services primarily financial institutions and large corporations would do well to have some of these courses in the bank. This is true even if your anticipated track is in litigation rather than transactions.

Any prospective business lawyer can gain a lot from basic courses in accounting, finance, corporate finance, securities, and banking. There's even an argument to be made that everyone going to law school should take a finance course. Like it or not, almost every attorney at some point in his practice encounters issues that can only be understood with a basic comprehension of interest rates, lending, capital accumulation, amortization, and credit.

Other Angles

If you really want to make your academic preparation for law school count, you'll have to venture beyond the popular prelaw departments.

One reason to take courses outside of the prelaw majors is that, with the exception of economics, they're simply not analytically-oriented enough, strictly speaking. Obviously, at the highest level in any field one is doing "analysis." But for exposure to the kind of analysis that lends itself to "legal thinking," history and political science are not the last word.

Thus we come to the uncomfortable subject we alluded to earlier: math and science. Anyone considering a legal practice in patent or technology-oriented law will have to be fluent in the substantive topics as well as law (so, too, with lawyers who deal in medical ethics, environmental law, or similar specialized fields).

Everyone would be better off knowing more math. It is analytical reasoning in its purest form; it is a model of everything and the language of all the sciences. Most colleges require at least a semester or two of science or math, because an educated person ought to know more than arithmetic.

Chances are that most people reading this book aren't good at math. They're actually kind of bad at it. They don't like it. So let's get to the point: Do the rest of us have to take calculus and physics in college?

No.

Everyone wants you to be as well-rounded as you can be, but there's no sense in going overboard. Many mathematics majors and physics majors and engineers have become great lawyers. And many social science, history, and literature majors take a few semesters of math and science and enjoy them.

But anyone asking whether she "has to" take courses in these subjects obviously doesn't want to. Unless you can take hard-core quantitative courses and do well on them or take them on a pass-fail basis (and pass!), they may cost you more trouble than they're worth. If math or science courses are going to throw your GPA for a loop, they're not worth it.

Does that mean you shouldn't take them? No. Law school admissions offices know that calculus and differential equations are harder subjects than Chinese pottery. If you get a C+ in math, you may be rewarded for your effort. It's not a completely unjust world.

That C+, however, will have a different effect on your GPA than an A in that pottery class. The effect will be negative. Even though admissions offices know which courses are which, your transcript will almost surely be examined only if you make certain numerical cutoffs (indices bases solely on your GPA and LSAT) as explained in chapter 10.

In sum, you can afford a few middling math grades, and in the long run they may pay off. Your hardiness will not go unappreciated by admissions officers, and, no less importantly, you'll learn some math and improve your analytical skills.

Across the Spectrum

It has been established here that any major done the right way can be a prelaw major, especially if it's a major where you can snag a 3.6 GPA.

There is a panoply of courses, however, whose usefulness in eventual legal study is more obvious. Whether or not they will be useful depends largely on which way you end up tacking in law school—toward business law, academia, civil rights, finance, criminal law, or whatever.

Here is a somewhat random sampling of subjects that are more obvious prelaw majors than philology, Basque literature, or vegetable studies, or in which an introductory course or two would almost certainly enhance your law school experience:

- Anthropology, the study of humankind, may well be applicable. Contrary to the litany of bad jokes out there, lawyers are human, and by far most of their clients are.

- Architecture is excellent preparation for many of the areas of law relating to space and structure, such as zoning and land use, construction law, environmental law.

- Chemistry is practically a "must" if you want to do certain kinds of patent work, as well as sophisticated environmental law. It could also be useful if you end up practicing in any other area of law related to the chemical and petroleum industries.

- Computer science is the subject that all of earth's eventual rulers will know. Even Mr. Gates needs lawyers.

- Engineering (all kinds), a combination of the theoretical and the practical in science, is a fantastic preparation for almost any field. An engineering degree virtually guarantees one a spot in the patent law firm of his choice.

- English and literature give you excellent writing training and also teach you about the world.

- Geology is very good for environmental law and, again, practice related to the vast petrochemical field.

- Philosophy is the place where you can learn formal logic on one end of the hallway and, on the other end, the political and legal philosophy of John Stuart Mill, H.L.A. Hart, and others. This subject, which is very demanding, is an excellent preparation for law school.

- Psychology can be a useful prelaw preparation, since it can acquaint you with issues relevant to criminal law, advocacy for the mentally ill, and your fellow lawyers.

- Sociology is a discipline that frequently intersects with the study of law. It's a good combination, since sociology is an approach to understanding social behavior and phenomena, and is a little less antiseptic than economics.

Far-Flung History

If you're interested in going beyond American history and take other-area history courses, the payoff in law school becomes attenuated. Certainly it's nice to have a background in European, especially English, history, especially in courses that are still solidly built on the common law, such as property, estates, and criminal law. If your orientation is toward "international" practice, you'll probably want to do area studies in history and political science that are related to those areas—and, of course, master a language or two. But these are extras.

This is not about political correctness; it's about knowledge. Knowing history may or may not predispose you toward conclusions on topics that arise in law school, but that's better than your predispositions being formed in ignorance or worse.

One Last Word

The only way to impress admissions officers and have any chance at success in law and law school is to learn how to write well.

Even political science and history may not be all that useful for this. You may do a lot of reading, but few of the specialists in these fields are truly good writers, especially contemporary ones. While reading the prose of Edward Gibbon and Abraham Lincoln is bound to improve your appreciation for language, the more recent variety of academic historical and political discourse, much less the quasi-English of the social sciences, will doom you to inscrutability. Hard-scientists and others taking quantitatively oriented courses need fear this effect less, but need practice writing more.

You need courses that stress writing, not merely as a medium for expressing ideas, but as a craft unto itself. Most colleges require at least one course in expository English in the English department. You should take more; fiction and non-fiction, English and the classics of other languages in translation. You must read the writing of writers; learn how to use words; how to shape sentences; and for Pete's sake you must learn exactly how to use a comma.

Literature courses will, besides exposing you to good writing, require you to do a lot of writing for yourself. The instructors will be focusing on your written expression, and with a little luck you'll achieve a level of literacy usually found only among pre-1960 graduates of American high schools.

Mastering English will aid you on the LSAT. It will help you on your essays for law school admission, on your law school exams, and in your legal writing course. And it will save you as you read judicial opinions, write briefs, argue motions, and draft correspondence. Your very thought processes will be improved by the exercise of undertaking to explain your thoughts clearly. You'll come to see that you cannot trust the thinking of anyone whose written language is obscure.

Learning to write, not only properly, but well, will enable you to stand among and stand out among lawyers. College is your last chance to spend real time on, and get professional attention for, your writing. Don't waste it.

CHAPTER EIGHT

The Not-So-Fast Track

Every law school requires a bachelor's degree. But none requires you to have gotten that degree the same year you start law school. So what's the rush?

There are many good reasons to take a breath and step off the fast track for a year, or two, or three before plunging into law school.

This is not to say that undergraduate readers should think about law as a second career or plan on going to law school nine years after graduating college. Very few people can realistically plan so far in advance. But for those of you who are sure, or almost sure, about attending law school, there's an argument to be made that, despite your certainty, you'd be better off cooling your heels for a year or two.

CUTTING YOURSELF A BREAK

What to do during this time? You could work. While you may want to go through the normal recruiting process, having law school as a near-term goal could allow you to relax about what kind of work you do. You might travel or win a fellowship or a "year abroad"-type exchange situation, even without still being in college. You might spend the year in an informal or otherwise non-career-oriented, educational program. You could even work as a paralegal and get an inside look at the profession you think you want to join.

The Protolegal

Some people work as paralegals for a year or two between college and law school. Is this a good idea?

On the one hand, spending time in a law office does demonstrate to application offices that you've really thought about and learned about at least a segment of the legal profession, that you're not starry-eyed about that dark beast called "the law," nor is your interest in it a passing fancy. Also, being a paralegal can be hard but very well-paying work. And you will learn a lot about the profession, which would put you way ahead of the reality curve of your classmates on that first day of law school.

On the other hand, being a paralegal is a very "prelaw" kind of thing to do, meaning: While working as a paralegal never hurt anyone's chances at getting into law school, it doesn't serve to distinguish you particularly, and it doesn't indicate much imagination. If anything, time spent in a big law firm only contributes to more of the "life = law = life" tunnel vision that taking time off is supposed to help you avoid. And in places where paralegal certification is required to work as a paralegal, the time spent in paralegal training will cost you money and slow your career course down.

The pluses and minuses are reflected in the experience of Craig Long, a law student who went to paralegal school after graduating from Gustavus Adolphus College in St. Peter, Minnesota. His interest in law school was first piqued as a freshman (then at Drake University in Des Moines), when he lived next door to the law school and studied in the law library. "Academic counselors [at Gustavus] were always willing to discuss law school, but their perceptions of the legal profession were often negative, and I began to have second thoughts about choosing law as a profession," he says. He decided that a law-related summer internship following his junior year would be a good way to find out more.

That summer, Long took a non-paying internship with a Minnesota county judge. "The clerks suggested that I take time off before school before making the commitment," he says, an option he had never considered before. One suggested becoming a legal assistant, which would enable him to work in the field without making the profound commitment of a legal education.

"I have to admit I was hesitant at first," says Long. "In my mind, being a paralegal was like settling for second best, and I wasn't sure I was willing to do that." But the chorus of law school graduates all around him convinced Long that, as he says, "I shouldn't go to law school unless I was 'absolutely' sure that that was what I wanted to do."

Long attended a paralegal training course, received American Bar Association certification, and got a job with a Minneapolis law firm through a temp agency. "My position carried little opportunity to exercise any independent decision-making and required little analytical thought." he said. "The projects I was assigned to while working as a paralegal rarely allowed me to utilize my education and could easily have been completed by a middle school student. This was true even after working for several months, and the senior paralegals didn't do much more than I did.

"On the other hand," continues Long, "the second-year law students [clerking in the firm] did the work I had expected to do, and they were paid at least five times what I was per week."

Were there any advantages to working as a paralegal before law school? "It provided me with the last bit of experience I needed to make up my mind before law school," says Long. But, he adds, "It might have been better if I had worked for a large corporation or as a financial analyst for several years before starting law school. My 'real world experiences' were focused entirely on the law. To be honest, I don't recommend becoming a paralegal at all—regardless of what the *Wall Street Journal* says about the profession in its articles about the job market."

Long, who ultimately did apply and get in to law school, admits that he did learn one important thing seeing the world of law firms from the inside: "I worked as a paralegal at a huge firm that employs literally thousands of attorneys across the nation and in Europe. The office politics, along with the impersonal atmosphere, drove me crazy. I never saw so much kissing up in my life. The younger associates often took drastic measures to impress partners, and that really turned me off.

"I hope," he concludes, "never to be part of a situation like that again."

Queuing Up

Different strategies will be necessary for different people in different situations. You may simply want to keep your hands off law school for now but work toward it during your "time off." Or you might want to identify law schools using the process described in chapter 10 but apply only to those that permit one- or two-year "deferrals" of admission. This way you can have the security of knowing you're going to law school as well as all the advantages discussed below.

The Personal Pluses

There are a few ways taking that break between college and law school could enhance your life:

- **Look before you leap.** Many people slide directly into law school, caught up in the application process or the frothy excitement of "being" something like a lawyer (as opposed to the nose-to-the-grindstone reality of practicing law for ten to fifty years). Taking time off ensures that you're not doing something hasty. In the interim, you can stay in touch with classmates who did make the leap and consider if you like what you see.

- **Avoid avoidance.** No one reading this is the "professional student" type; people who are just terrorized at the thought of leaving school—right? After all, law school is one of the dumbest places there is to practice this "profession." It's expensive. There are, for all practical purposes, no merit-based grants, much less fellowships, for law students. And, with its grueling, mandatory first-year course load, law school is much more unpleasant than signing up for a masters in "leisure studies" or some such.

- **Walk a mile in your own moccasins.** The unfortunate truth is that for the vast majority of us, the college experience has only a passing resemblance to adulthood. If, as someone once said, high school is just subsidized dating, college is something immensely scarier or perhaps sillier. When you begin law school, you're getting on a highway that, for most people, has few exit ramps. Why not find out what it's like to be an adult before committing your entire adulthood to the legal profession?

- **A few grey hairs.** Once you're in law school, it adds a little heft to your classroom presentation, not to mention your relationship with professors, to have done something in your life besides sit and take notes. A little exposure to "real life" (i.e., living somewhere other than in your parents' house or a dorm; pulling a full-time job; sweating the rent) will enhance your understanding of the social and personal situations underlying some legal disputes and policy debates.

- **Money in the bank.** If you're capable of earning more than a subsistence income in your time off, you may be able to sock away some money for school or buy a car or some other asset that you won't be able to get while a student. (But see below about the financial-aid risks of this.)

- **See Paris.** If law school seems almost certain, know this: Whatever nutty thing it is you've always wanted to do—bust broncos, join a zydeco band, learn Talmud in Jerusalem—this is certainly your best chance to do it. Though some larger law firms will give deferred starting dates to special recruits, it's not so they can go on some lark; typically, it's to work as a judicial clerk or perhaps finish off some graduate work. Once you're out of law school, you'll have a hard time explaining those six post-graduation months on a Peruvian coca farm when you start looking for work. Though there are exceptions, generally unconventional career paths don't appeal to conventional people. Lawyers are very conventional people.

The Strategic Upside

Besides all the life-enhancing reasons listed above, there are some hard, cold reasons why you might want to chill out for a year or two:

Declaring Independence

Depending on the formulas used at different schools, you could make a few bucks on your law school financial aid package merely by scuba diving for two years. (No, not two years straight.) This may be enough time to truly rend you from your parents' money, or perhaps to rend your parents' money from you, and convince your school that you're truly independent. That could mean a substantial tuition reduction depending on the schools' resources. The trick, of course, is to make just enough money to live on and perhaps to buy a car or some other middling-sized assets but not to accumulate enough that you risk being told to cough it up for your "expected contribution"—all the while not taking any substantial aid from home.

Gilding the Lily

Let's say you're not as strong an academic candidate as you'd like to be. Who is? It's a general rule that the further you are from college, the less your college performance matters for admissions. (How much less depends on the school and the amount of time.) You could spend a year or two at getting some academic degree, which will both enhance your academic seriousness and demonstrate your ability to do good work at the graduate level.

Gilding the Lily, Part II

The other alternative to enhancing your profile through post-college activity is to invest it in some non-academic demonstration of seriousness. It may be a public-service or career-oriented job. The latter imparts maturity and helps make your law school choice look more considered, something schools do appreciate. Working in public service is more politically correct, which certain schools might appreciate even more.

The Greatest Love of All

Considering that the cohort of college-age people is rapidly shrinking, as is the interest in attending law school, your admissions chances probably increase at many schools as time goes on.

Just Do It

Or not. There is a substantial body of opinion that says, if you've reached whatever cutoff point you need for certainty about law school, get on with it. Just as there are numerous reasons to take a break, there are almost as many reasons to stay on track.

The Personal Minuses

- **Not getting any younger.** If you're going to end up practicing law either way, why waste time? By going straight through, you can get on the seven-year partner track when you're 25 instead of 27. If, after five years, you make a career change or an employment change, wouldn't you rather make it at 30 than at 33?

- **Opportunity cost.** Financially speaking, there's not much benefit from two years of surfing the Himalayas or collecting Depression glass. If you're getting on the legal career track anyway, why give up two years of lost income?

- Keep in mind that lost income isn't measured by your salary at the beginning of your career, but at the end. That is, all things being equal, economists assume you'll retire at a set age. If you hit, say, 65 at a point where your seniority is x, you'll earn less than if you hit 65 at a point where your seniority is x-2. Even if your salary is stable from age 60 until retirement, you'll have two more years to accumulate it if you've started two years earlier—and with that calculus, add on everything that goes with accumulation of more income, such as money earned from that income (investments and savings).

- **Time marches on.** You might put your legal career on hold, but the rest of the world keeps spinning, schlepping you along with it. If, all things being equal, you get married at age 28 and have your first child at age 31, at what stage would you rather be in your legal career? The answer is almost certainly "the latest stage possible," since law school is harder first year, and law practice is harder (usually) in the earlier years, and so on. Of course, all things are never equal, and some people will make their personal plans depend on their careers, not vice versa. Even then, having more years "ahead of you" makes the planning easier. No one wants to have to juggle a lot of commitments at once.

- **Old dogs, old tricks.** Being a student is a state of mind, one which some people find hard to recapture once they stop. While in college, especially if you're shooting for law school, you're apt to be "cooking" academically. Getting back into a studying mood might be hard after a couple of years of not having to crack a book.

- **Think about this reason tomorrow.** Procrastinators should definitely watch out here. If you're the kind of person who, failing to do something immediately, simply fails to do it ever, perhaps you should strike while the iron is hot and take advantage of your ambitious humor.

The Strategic Downside

To some extent, the "strategic" downside to taking time off is identifiable with the "personal" downside. No one gets extra credit on any admissions office index for not taking time off. But there are some other angles:

Time is Money

During your time off you could work for a subsistence wage, a higher wage that will enable you to live comfortably and not save, or a lot of money. Subsistence existence is no fun, except perhaps in retrospect; if you haven't tried it, there's little romance in dodging debt-collector phone calls. Making a lot of money almost certainly means that the law school financial aid office will try to get to that money when you get your financial aid package. While there's no reason to be ashamed of financing more of your own education than you otherwise would, some say there is no shame either in letting an endowment fund designed for the purpose help you out. As for the "live comfortably" option, you may be surprised when you discover that the financial aid office thinks you lived a tad too comfortably, and tries to "reach" income that long ago was sunk into CDs, a laser printer, or Samuel Adams Lager.

Your Time and Their Money

Your parents' financial planning may be affected by your decision on when to attend law school. Maybe your folks would like to finish their tuition-financing gig a little bit earlier than your life-exploration schedule would otherwise indicate. Maybe they'd like to know you're done with your educational odyssey so that they can take that cruise they've been waiting for. It's also possible that you won't achieve financial-aid "independence" by skiing Aspen for two years, and that could affect their planning too.

The Price Was Right

So far, the trend in favor of rising tuition hasn't slowed down. The price of a law degree is increasing faster than inflation. Obviously, it's better to get on the train before the fare goes up.

The More Things Change

It will get easier to get into a law school as the years go by. It will not be any easier to get into Harvard, Yale, Stanford, or any of the other most desirable schools.

ON YOUR OWN

The decision about whether to go straight to law school or take time off is ultimately very personal. It depends on your situation in life. Just do your best to make sure that whichever way you come out, it's the best thing you can do for yourself.

And remember: almost every law school lets you take a breather if you want one. Doing so is a little more radical than taking time off right after college, but it has the advantage of nailing down that commitment, at least a little of it. If you're unsure about your commitment to being a lawyer, the fact that you're a semester into it doesn't mean you have to throw good money after bad. And even if you are sure of your commitment, you still might want one last shot at seeing Paris.

CHAPTER NINE

Choosing a Law School

Does it make a lot of difference what law school you go to?
Yes.

Given that answer, is which law school you go to the most important decision you have to make?
No.

The most important decisions you have to make at this point are the ones addressed in the previous eight chapters. After analyzing yourself, your talents, your desires and ambitions, and applying that analysis to what you've learned about the legal profession, you have to make the much more important decision of whether you want to be a lawyer. There is no law school on earth that, by virtue of admitting you, will make a bad career choice a good career choice; though there are three very narrow exceptions that punch a hole or two in that last statement.

A Caveat

This chapter discusses law schools, and the premise of this discussion is that some law schools are "better," and others are "worse." For all practical purposes, these terms mean "better" or "worse" for you. There are some people who, either because of their goals, their politics, or their temperament, wouldn't appreciate the benefit of a Yale Law School education even if it were offered to them.

There are few absolutes in comparing law schools. And more importantly, there are few differences among the many schools that will enable a well-prepared, strategically-oriented person to get the legal education and legal credential she wants.

Almost all law schools that are accredited by the ABA do in fact offer a fine legal education. Because of the ABA's requirements for facilities, curricular offerings, and other areas affecting law school quality, law schools have gotten better and better. Plus, schools are in a constant race to move upward in "the rankings"—motivated by the desire to attract better-quality students as well as financial support from alumni and the local legal community. Finally, considering the competition for permanent, much less tenured, positions on law school faculties, almost every law school has some very, very talented law teachers.

This whole discussion, then, should be kept in perspective. The main point of it is to be sure of what you want in a law school and to go about the most logical way of getting it (or getting as close to it as possible).

The Troika

No one with an official paid position in the world of legal education would ever be caught dead going on the record with this information, but there are, in fact, a few top law schools that are exceptions to the rule. In no particular order, the exceptions are the "big three" of law schools—the Troika: Harvard, Yale, and Stanford.

Many of the great schools of this country join these three as "the very best" law schools in terms of reputation. By virtual acclamation other "tip-top" schools include the University of Chicago and Columbia University. A law firm that sees any of these names on a resume is going to pay that resume extra attention.

But the Troika is different. These three names travel beyond the legal profession. They are tickets to instant credibility, deserved or otherwise, in virtually any establishment or academic environment. They are, frankly, magic.

Stanford, Yale, and Harvard degrees are not lifetime guarantees of wealth or employment, mind you. There are some circumstances where they're not even ideal for legal job hunting. A law review member at the University of Texas will probably get the nod over an otherwise equivalent Yalie for a top Houston position. Strange as it may seem, Stanford's name doesn't resonate in the Ivy League bastions of the East the way Harvard's and Yale's do. And few Harvard students will say that a Harvard degree is even a guarantee of much of a legal education, what with that school's famed political polarization, faculty ego wars, and hyper-competitive 600-person classes.

But if there's any circumstance where the bestowal of benefit of the doubt can help a person—in business, in politics, in satellite fields to law practice such as legal media, and especially teaching—Troika J.D.s help like nothing else does.

Perspective: Of the hundred-thousand or so people who will take the LSAT this year, maybe 1,500 will be offered the opportunity to attend one or more of the Troika schools. Virtually all who are accepted have grade-point averages around 3.8, and LSATs above the 95th percentile.

If you are one of the lucky few who can garner admission to one of these law schools, it hardly matters what you want to do after graduation. This book stresses the importance of thinking hard about the decision to attend law school. But if you're invited to join the Troika, it makes sense for almost everyone who doesn't want to be a doctor or a physicist to just accept. Don't even think about it.

Okay, Starry Eyes, Back to Work

That said about the Troika, let's now get back to the rest of us.

If anyone tells you it doesn't matter where you go to law school, ignore them. It matters, regardless of your plans and ambitions and sense of self-worth. It matters despite the fact that the academic offerings from law school to law school differ only in a handful of ways. And it matters even though in some cases it shouldn't.

There are several factors that will determine which is the best law school for you. Once you have worked them out for yourself, you can proceed to chapter 10, which is about the admissions game. As always, however, the approach here is to identify the target before pulling an arrow from the quiver. The factors are:

- Cost
- Geography
- Placement
- Reputation
- Faculty
- Curriculum

- Quality of life
- Facilities

These will be considered in the order given, but the order is quite artificial, especially since these factors can be interrelated, as the first discussion—ostensibly about money—will demonstrate. It is up to you to prioritize these factors; the mission here is to flesh them out.

Cost

The economics of paying for law school have been painfully addressed in chapter 6. Here is where we jump from theory to practice.

You may choose to, or you may have to, attend the cheapest law school there is. Maybe there's no way you can make it with the financial aid package you've been offered; maybe you don't want to accept financial aid; maybe you don't want to borrow tons of money. All these are good reasons to consider going to the cheapest law school—taken by themselves.

We'll accept as a given, for now, the premise that you want to attend the least expensive law school. The problem, however, is that any law school is not necessarily better than no law school. It may be worse. Or it may be just fine.

Let's say the cheapest law school you get into is Bob's All-Night Law School Bar and Grill, or BANLSBAG. BANLSBAG is simply not a well-regarded law school. It's not just at the bottom of the list; it's not even on the list. Does it make sense to go there? There are two main questions at this juncture of the analysis:

- **Accreditation.** First off, if it's not an ABA-approved school, it probably doesn't matter how little you pay. Virtually no state (California being the notable exception) is going to let you sit for its bar exam without ABA accreditation. The fact that the state the school is in may accredit the school for its own bar is nice, but how can you be sure you'll never want your law degree to count outside of that state? You can't be sure. Even if you have some plan which includes getting a legal education but never practicing, you should not want to make a three-year-long investment in law school that can't at least be upgraded to a law license in any state.

- **Your goal.** Accreditation is just the first step in finding out if a prospective law school is capable of providing you with the credentials you seek. If your dream is to be a legal Master of the Universe, planning out great strategies in your office at Century City, LaSalle Street, or Park Avenue, Bob's simply won't get you there, period, stop. A BANLSBAG degree is incompatible with your goal, and three years spent there will simply be wasted for you. Hard fact, but true. On the other hand, what if you've been selling insurance for five years, and you'd like to add a law degree so you can top off your estate planning work with will drafting? What if your family business wants to send someone to law school to bring a little expertise in house? What if you're an engineer whose corporate employer is willing to pay half the cost of a law degree so you can come back to the company as a patent lawyer? Then BANLSBAG might be just the ticket. The point is, a bargain can be a bargain or a bust. Half-off on dog food is no bargain if you've got a cat.

The answer, then, is that it's possible that the cheapest law school could be good enough for you. Just make sure that (1) it's accredited, or at least has accreditation pending, and that (2) on the most fundamental level, you can accomplish your legal-education goals with a degree from that school.

In the Long Run

Now let's reconsider this idea of saving money in the first place. This is not a novel point, but it is worth focusing on for a minute or two. It may be very expensive even to go to a cheap law school.

An extreme, almost absurd, example: What if placement information indicates that BANLSBAG alumni typically land jobs paying an average of $22,000? Whereas you are also invited to attend Enormous State University's school of law (ESU), albeit at a cost that's $30,000 more than BANLSBAG's over three years. But most ESU alumni get jobs making $48,000 as first-years. In a couple of years, you could pay off all or most of that $30,000 (plus any interest) just with the difference between the $22,000 job and the $48,000 job. And, of course, if you agree to sign on that dotted line and attend the elite Ivory Tower College of Law, you may have to run up $40,000 in debt. But most Ivory Tower babies slide into Wall Street positions paying $80,000. One year, and you're debt free.

Now, the above example has a few logical flaws, some of which are:

- Maybe you don't want the kind of work that pays $80,000 and aren't willing to mortgage your future to get it.

- Maybe you know yourself well enough to realize that you won't pay $15,000 down or, as in the Ivory Tower case, the whole nut in one year. Given $80,000, you'll spend every penny you can.

- No law school can guarantee a starting salary to any, much less all, of its graduates.

But the general idea should be clear: As Ben Franklin (who, by the way, would've made a great patent lawyer if he were around today) used to say, don't be penny-wise and pound-foolish. Some things are worth paying for, even borrowing for. If you've concluded that you want that law career and know where you want to go with it, you should sit down and figure out what you're prepared to pay to get the opportunities offered you. Remember that cheapness is very different from value.

PLACEMENT AND GEOGRAPHY

"Placement," of course, is bureaucratese for "getting a job." If you've read this far, then you should understand that law school is for people who want to be lawyers. So, any law school that can't "close the deal" and help you get from law school graduate to practicing law isn't doing its job.

Keep in mind that, as the discussion works its way up to national schools, the focus in this section is on placement, not quality, value, or any other inherent good. Those are discussed elsewhere in this chapter.

National, Regional and Local

This is as good a place as any to introduce the concepts of the national, regional, and local law schools. Though these terms are relevant to considerations such as prestige, first and foremost they speak to how broadly a school's graduates are recruited.

Do you want to work in your home state? Or anywhere but your home state? Do you aspire to big-city practice, or would you be happy to settle in a small community where virtually every member of the county bar knows each other? Or do you want to have the most options possible? Do you mind attending a top-five school that just happens to be in a high-crime zone? Answering these questions will take you well along the way to narrowing your search for the right law school.

All Politics Is Local

"Local" law schools, as the name implies, are those whose best placement successes are in the immediate city or, in some cases, the state in which they're located. In a way, "local" is a euphemism for "not-so-well-known" (or worse), but this in itself shouldn't deter you. One reason is that most law schools are, frankly, "local." A second reason is that, while there are no doors a local degree can open that a national or regional degree can't, local can be quite a sufficient little place.

An excellent example is Newark, New Jersey's Seton Hall University School of Law. Beyond New Jersey, Seton Hall is known, if at all, for its basketball program, notwithstanding the school's recent upgrade to state-of-the-art facilities and a number-two ranking in a Princeton Review/National Jurist magazine "student satisfaction" poll based on faculty, facilities, and quality of life (see Appendix). Eighty percent of Seton Hall's nearly fourteen hundred students are from New Jersey; virtually all will (eventually) work in New Jersey after graduation. Nationally, the only school that places a higher percentage of its graduates in judicial clerkships is a much smaller one in New Haven, Connecticut.

Seton Hall works for New Jersey residents, or those who would be New Jersey residents and want to work there. It is true that the growth of legal jobs in Northeastern states such as New Jersey has slowed; there have been twice as many law school graduates as legal job openings in recent years. It is also true that few Seton Hall graduates are offered positions in the elite northern New Jersey firms, which recruit primarily from New York schools and Rutgers, the state school also located in Newark. And only the most exceptional Seton Hall students make use of their degrees beyond the Hudson and Delaware Rivers.

But the school's alumni are absorbed into the New Jersey legal community. To be a Seton Hall graduate in New Jersey is to be part of a local but important network that makes up the meat and potatoes of an important state bar. Seton Hall is a local success story.

There's one more big difference between national/regional law schools and local law schools: Local law schools prepare you for the bar exam.

That may be good or bad. Skeptics say some law schools are nothing more than three-year bar-review courses and point out that legal education should be more than preparation for a test. The lesser-known schools are supposedly motivated by the desire to trumpet their high pass rates.

On the other side of the fence are theory-heavy institutions (usually found at the dizzying heights of the rankings). There, the legend goes, study of something as mundane as black-letter legal rules is supposedly eschewed, and law schools like Yale are notorious for producing more than their share of first-time bar failures.

Even if it's true (no one really knows), does it matter? Look at it this way: Everyone has to pass the bar exam. But, ultimately, every lawyer does. It would be a shame, and probably a long-term loss, for a law student to not be exposed to a little bit of depth in his education. On the other hand, no one's ever heard of a University of Chicago graduate pumping gas for want of passing the bar exam.

The Smallest Region

Evaluating the ins and outs of legal recruiting in New York is a topic unto itself. New York is the legal capital of the world. There is no law school that is not represented, and probably more than once, somewhere in the confines of the Empire State. This representation, however, does not a "national school" make, or virtually every school would rightfully claim to be a national school. Gotham is simply a national and international crossroads for law practice; as in everything else, among the most ambitious, most talented, and most nutty specimens of any group, a large percentage find their way to the City Whose Lawyers Never Sleep.

Your ambition may well be to practice in one of the great New York law firms, many of which stand astride the world of commerce. It is undoubtedly the single most exciting, well-paying, and challenging place to practice law. It is also clearly the rudest, hardest, and most frustrating.

But if "The City" is the Big Apple of your eye, you should see how well each school you are considering has placed is graduates there. Ultimately, however, New York is not so different from Washington, Los Angeles or California: If you don't go to a national school, a regional (Mid-Atlantic) regional school, or a local (New York City) school, it could be tough sledding breaking into the New York big time.

Across the Fruited Plain

A "regional" school is one whose placement influence extends beyond the immediate city or state. Its name is well-known and, to some extent or another, respected in a whole geographical market. Almost inevitably a regional school pretends to have "national" status, since, by virtue of its regional cachet, it is nationally known. But regional schools are distinguishable from the "true" national schools in that you find few of their graduates practicing outside the region.

These zones may be broadly identified as the traditional geographic "regions" of the Northeast, the Midwest, the Southeast (or South Atlantic), the South (the southern states not bordering the eastern seaboard), the Southwest, and the West Coast. The Northeast may also be broken down into two smaller regions, namely New England and the Mid-Atlantic. Though there are other geographic schemes, these sufficiently reflect the extent of the respective regions' "legal geography."

In terms of placement, a regional school can accomplish everything a local school can and more. It is usually more competitive, in terms of admissions, than a local school. Is there any reason to attend a regional school over a national school? Absolutely. Regional schools often trump national schools, especially locally. In other words, some national schools from outside the region may pack less placement punch, at least in the short run, than the right regional school.

Thus, if you want to work in New Orleans, you'll do better attending Tulane University, one of the top law schools in the South, than New York University. A Boston University degree, respected throughout the Northeast, will probably do you more good in Boston than a J.D. from Northwestern. A Baylor grad may have the inside track in much of Texas over a Cornell alumnus.

The *Princeton Review Student Access Guide to the Best Law Schools* is the most appropriate place to learn how different schools fit into different regions; it also analyzes the respective regions (though broken up in a slightly different manner than in the above paragraph) and discusses the respective schools. If you have a good sense of where you want to end up as an attorney, you may also have a sense of which regional schools have influence there. Certainly, if you are attending or have attended college in the given region, you should have no trouble developing through the grapevine as well as in your college placement office a sense of who's who.

Ultimately, keep in mind again that law schools routinely report the regions where their graduates have been placed, and use that information. It's the truest test of how much punch a given degree has in the resume race.

The National League

Let's all sit down before we discuss the topic of "national schools." It can get kind of emotional. Remember the caveat from the beginning of this chapter: Among ABA-approved law schools, you're unlikely to get an inadequate legal education. Among "better" schools, the education is even more valuable. All the schools that are even in the running for "regional" or "national" status have outstanding faculties, excellent reputations, and provide fine legal educations.

A "national" school is one that rings a bell almost anywhere in the country. It is one that virtually everyone in the profession, no matter where, has heard of. It follows from this that the schools regarded as national schools are often the most difficult to get into; which, in turn, makes them even more desirable. In other words, the discussion here is about renown.

There are national schools, and there are national schools. Some are national, in the sense described above, but still have most influence in their immediate region. The phenomenon is similar to the regional vs. national one discussed above. Thus, if you want to practice law in Texas, the University of Texas may well make more sense than the University of California at Los Angeles or the University of Pennsylvania.

Of course, there is the Troika, the untouchable top three of Harvard, Yale, and Stanford. These are the three schools you probably want to go to even if their regional influence is somewhat attenuated, just because they're so . . . so Harvard, Yale, and Stanford. (On the other hand, if you live in Texas and really, really know you want to be a Dallas oil lawyer, it would be hard to turn down the bargain of a U of T education just to snag some fancy-pants degree from one of the top three.)

Beyond the Big Three are a couple of other schools that get universal resume respect throughout the country. As mentioned earlier, these are the University of Chicago and Columbia University. They don't necessarily have the same impact outside the profession as the other three, but you could say these five schools make up the "top five," and many people do say that.

From this point on, it gets shaky. Though there are many different versions of the "Top 10" (or 15 or 20), the other law schools most commonly deemed national schools include all the Ivy League law schools; Big Ten standouts such as Michigan (Ann Arbor), Illinois (Champagne-Urbana), Minnesota (Twin Cities), Iowa, and Northwestern; other great state or state-affiliated schools such as Texas, the University of Virginia, California (Berkeley; some say UCLA, some say USC, and some say both); as well as New York University, Georgetown, Duke, and Vanderbilt.

As you can imagine, personal and regional prejudice often inform these characterizations—and that's the whole point. As for choosing a national school for other purposes, whether for your ego or your long-term career plans, we continue below.

Another Awful Truth

"'After your first job,' they told me, 'all they care about is what you've done, not where you went to school.' What a bunch of baloney!" So says Henry Jacobson, a veteran of the 1990-91 New York legal-layoff depression. Jacobson, who graduated from New York University in 1988, had flopped out at New York's high-flying Kaye, Scholer, Fierman, Hays & Handler, and needed to find new work, fast.

"The headhunters all wanted to know if I'd done law review at NYU, which I hadn't," he says. "I'm sitting on the other end, thinking, 'What happened to being at Kaye, Scholer?'" Jacobson had actually been eligible for law review and, in a rush of rashness, passed it up on the belief that once employed by a top Park Avenue firm (as he was early in his law school career), he was "set for life." Bad advice.

"Here I was, out of law school for four years, and the recruiting coordinators and headhunters wanted transcripts. You think I was thinking of that the spring of my third year?"

Ultimately, Jacobson landed in a large New Jersey firm. "The Jersey firms, at least at that point, weren't asking for transcripts from Manhattan refugees," Jacobson says. "They didn't have the slightest interest in how much document production (reviewing boxes full of paper in giant cases) I'd done in New York. But they saw Princeton, my undergraduate school, and NYU, and decided to give me the benefit of the doubt. The hiring partner said, 'I don't care if you screwed up the last time, because I believe we can turn you around if you've got the raw material. And it looks here like you've got the raw material.' I wasn't going to argue."

REPUTATION

While the knives are out, the "reputation" issue must be dealt with, to the extent it hasn't already. Reputation here means "prestige." This word gets some people nervous. Again, the attempt is to drain this issue of emotion before addressing it. This is not about fairness or justice, but what is called in Yiddish a metzius—a situation that just *is*, the way you find it.

Reputation is not only something that you get from a "fancy" school; but you do get more of it there. Still, even in the most locally-oriented milieu, there are gradations of reputation and prestige that can matter and that may be very much under your control when the time comes to accept an offer of enrollment.

One function of reputation, which was artificially labeled "renown" above, is its effect on placement. There are other reasons for being concerned (or not) about getting into the school with the best possible reputation.

Down the Road

The epoch during which people retired at age 65 from the company or firm where they first started is long gone. In fact, career-switching, must less firm-switching, is hardly even noteworthy.

Your choice of law school should reflect this, but it cuts two ways: On the one hand, if you leave the law completely and end up in the touring company of "Grease," it absolutely doesn't matter where you went to law school. On the other hand, if you want to eventually move into an area that is allied, whether loosely or closely, with the law, the more burnished your degree, the better. This includes the case whereby you decide to get an MBA or another professional or graduate degree. Admissions offices are staffed by admissions officers, who are simply people. A more prestigious resume is just going to be more helpful than a lesser one.

All this leads to a powerful a fortiori argument: If a prestigious law degree is helpful outside the legal profession, how much more so is it helpful if you change tracks inside the legal profession? Again, forget about that first job and think about the long term: When you want or need to change firms, your resume will once again be examined. Your past work experience will be important, but these days so many people have had so much similar early work experience in law that it can't tell the hiring person much. Any prestige that you purchase from your law school will come in quite handy.

All the more does this apply if you really change tracks and decide to try to become a judge, or a prosecutor, or a professor. Because at that point your past work experience becomes even less relevant. "Yes," they'll say, "She has quality accomplishments, the achievement of excellence, and is virtuous too. But can she also accomplish and achieve in this new context?" And for some reason, a little bit of Ivy creeping up that resume's margins make it seem a little more likely that she can. Ultimately, the law school reputation game is not about achievement, but about opening doors.

Feed Your Head

Be honest with yourself about your attitude toward prestige. If you don't care about it at all—really, not just something you're saying to seem chilled—you are among the lucky ones. It's like a gift, a freedom from tyranny. If that's you, you don't have to worry about this section. Choosing a law school solely to gratify your ego (much less your mom's) is a hell of a dumb way to choose a law school.

It might, however, be a perfectly reasonable way to accommodate your ego. It has to be fed, too. And given the arguments above, what's the worse thing that can happen? So you go to Duke to satisfy your ego. When it's over, you've got a Duke degree. That's not so bad. What is bad, though, would be getting a Duke law degree to satisfy a need for a "fancy" degree, when you really don't want to go to law school at all.

The trick, of course, is to balance your ego with your other, more practical, more mature, logical, farsighted, and economical drives. Part of this balance requires opening up your ego to feedback from the world of reality. That is, don't let your ego demand more than the world at large demands, given that the world at large is concerned plenty with prestige. Your ego might get hung up on attending the school "ranked" forty-sixth over the one "ranked" fifty-eighth, even though the second one is cheaper, prettier, and further from your parents' house. You should tell your ego that no one on earth cares about that distinction between forty-six and fifty-eight. Tell your ego to shut up so you can think.

There's one more trick. Work this stuff out before applying, not after. Once you get in to a school that no part of you but your ego thinks you should attend, the ego will have the upper hand. You'll be lost as soon as you see that beautiful, flattering, bond-stationery congratulatory letter from the Dean of Admissions herself. Remember, Emerald City was an awfully cool place to visit, but Dorothy and her friends had their mission mapped out before they hit the poppy fields. You'd be wise to do the same.

All That Glitters

All this go-for-the-prestige stuff is meant to be cautionary and to impart a message your prelaw advisor and the usual-suspect prelaw guides don't have the nerve to tell you. But it isn't a drop-dead, all-or-nothing deal. Just as a slight antidote to what's preceded, consider the following:

- *There are legal superstars, even at the highest and stuffiest levels of the profession, who didn't go to fancy law schools. And there will always be a handful of them.*

- *There are high-earning lawyers in every level of the profession who didn't go to fancy law schools, and there will always be quite a few of them.*

- *There are happy and content attorneys both in and out of practice who didn't go to fancy law schools, and, believe it or not, there will always be a lot of them.*

The prestige race is similar to what was said in the beginning of this book regarding "talent" vs. "ambition": There is a set of odds out there, and you may or may not

*like the way they're stacked. But if you want something
badly enough, there's no telling where your drive can
take you.*

FACULTY

Most undergraduates don't understand enough about the legal profession, the study of law, and their own professional future to really evaluate a law school faculty academically. One of the silliest scenes in "The Paper Chase" is where the protagonist, Hart, spews forth the well-known legal and academic accomplishments of the godlike Professor Kingsfield, all of which Hart has evidently assimilated in his naïve, rural, prelaw existence. Maybe Harvard 1L's really do look that kind of stuff up. But in real life, most legal academic resumes pretty much look the same.

The law faculties at most schools are made up of the best graduates of that school, usually after a judicial clerkship and perhaps a few years in practice, as well as a selection from a handful of national schools (inevitably including Harvard). Information available to you will bombard you with the names of impressive-sounding publications, from law review articles to textbooks. Indeed, most tenured law faculty members are pretty impressive specimens.

There may be slight differences in emphasis that are discernible from official admissions materials. Schools with a big "practical" or clinical philosophy may have more practically experienced faculty. That doesn't necessarily make them better teachers, but you may very well want to hear from someone who's been where you're going.

You can keep your ear to the ground by doing footwork at the school itself, as well as looking at published information, about certain faculty issues. Let's take a look at these:

Politics

Some law schools are driven by faculty dissension over politics, which often spills into student life. Whether it's affirmative action, the male-female tenure ratio, Critical Legal Studies, or abortion, law school faculties do tend to get caught up in things. When it stimulates discussion and learning, political ferment can be great. But when students become pawns in faculty power plays, everyone loses. If you hear about this stuff, mark it down as a demerit. Find out whether faculty politics are under control and what the prospects are for the future.

And by all means, if you learn that a campus has a particularly vigorous "thought police"—either in terms of intimidating unpopular viewpoints from being heard in class, or a "speech code" that regulates politically incorrect utterances, or any other intolerance of different ideology (be it of the right or the left)—avoid it like the plague. You won't become much of a lawyer if you're trained in an environment that stifles free expression, and once you get out there, there'll be no kangaroo courts to protect you from it.

Schools of Thought

Many law faculties are liberal, oriented to social action, protest, and challenging the system. Others are bastions of conservative ideology, with close ideological and personal ties to the corporate and financial worlds. But political debates don't have to become battlefronts to have an impact on your law school experience. They can also strongly inform the way law is taught.

Some law professors are enamored of economics-driven approaches to legal analysis, such as Law and Economics, made famous by professors like Richard Posner at the University of Chicago (now a federal appeals court judge). Others take to positively subversive analytical modes such as Critical Legal Studies, whose proponents include Duncan Kennedy of Harvard and Stanford. Leading scholars such as Posner and Kennedy set the terms of debates that faculty around the country love to jump in on.

You might want to challenge yourself and go against your natural flow, and that's an admirable thought. But realize that you could end up grinding your teeth to dust listening to three years of a thinly-disguised ideology that drives you nuts.

In reality, the problem isn't nearly as stark as the above would suggest. Not every faculty is either polarized or monolithic. Beware of gross over-generalizations like "all the faculty here are a bunch of [insert political epithet here]." Few law schools are really all that homogenous. You'll learn the most and the best by mixing and matching, which is what you can do in most places. Just make sure your prospective law schools are among those places.

Legal Writes

Who's teaching the students? Sometimes it is students. One of the most important courses you'll take in law school is legal writing. In that course, you'll learn not only how to write legal memoranda and briefs but also the research skills that will take you through the early years of your career. Yet some schools relegate the teaching of this critical course to none other than third-year law students, perhaps those with law review experience, but ultimately people who have absolutely no right to teach at the graduate level. This is a negative.

Though few law schools have more than one full-time faculty member assigned responsibility for legal writing (usually the director of the program), you should at least be taught by adjunct faculty, i.e., professionals. These are usually practitioners who have achieved some sort of distinction in academic publishing or practice. Unfortunately, the selection process for legal writing positions is itself often irregular, almost arbitrary. And information about it is seldom easy to get. But find out what you can and think very hard about whether you want to be taught by teachers or students.

Counting Heads

One more thing you want to know about the faculty: How many of them are there, compared to students? Student-faculty ratios are revealing. If they're too high, you know you're going to be in for big lectures, limited course offerings, and less access to profs than you probably would like. They can never be too low, though don't be fooled; some schools' faculty populations are swollen by large clinical programs.

While you're at it, try to determine how many of the faculty are full-time, as opposed to adjunct. A nice mix of adjunct faculty is fine, but some schools rely on them heavily as a way to subsidize the full-timers. Adjuncts, after all, usually get paid so little for their work that their teaching salaries are more properly characterized as honoraria. It's a cheap way to bulk up the faculty. But few adjuncts do much, if any, research. Though they bring fresh and abundant experience to the table, they can't, as a rule, bring as much depth or preparation as those who are engaged full-time in legal scholarship.

CURRICULUM

The world of legal education is in the midst of a debate that may have more impact on how law is taught than anything in the previous century. The question is, to put it very broadly: Should law schools focus on theory or practice? Many leaders in the legal world, including Stanford's Dean Brest and Robert MacCrate, (the latter being a former president of the American Bar Association), have called for an increased emphasis on skill-development as opposed to the well-honed craft of teaching doctrine and analysis.

At resource-rich schools such as Stanford, one approach to this perceived gap has been the development of "complementary curricula," designed to foster the kinds of skills lawyers need through interdisciplinary study. Another approach is to add more clinical education, i.e., hands-on "learning by doing," either in simulated settings or in training-wheel-type exposure to real-world counseling and advocacy.

Not everyone is enamored of the shift to skills development. No defender of the ancien régime (what the actor who played Professor Kingsfield in "The Paper Chase" would call "the old-fashioned way") would disagree with enhancing legal education with interdisciplinary education. But many question whether clinical education, taken beyond a certain point, is the correct role for law schools.

To some extent, this nattering negativity may be plain old stick-in-the-mudism. Opponents say that it's expensive and, for those who are new to it, disorienting to set up a clinical program. They also bring an element of snobbiness to their resistance: "This is not a trade school." These aren't good reasons for resisting the trend.

But there is an argument that law school is indeed the place to learn doctrine and analysis, and that skills can and should be picked up in the marketplace. (Remember; law firms claim they have to teach skills no matter how much clinical work a new associate has done in law school.)

The best of all possible worlds is, of course, a law school that offers lots of everything. More and more "old fashioned," prestigious names in law are offering meaningful clinical programs. If you can have all the options, there's no reason not to take them. If you have to choose, however, between a school that offers more clinics and one that doesn't, you'll have to decide how important that is to you. That will depend on the kind of self-assessment you've done (as discussed in the beginning of the book), at least in terms of whether you see yourself as a litigator, a transactions person, a generalist, or whatever, and in the milieu (big firm, small firm, government, etc.) you're most likely to take up your practice.

Ultimately, you should talk to lawyers who can advise you about their clinical experience and how worthwhile it actually was to them. But remember that their experience might not translate to a plan of action for you. There's no question that some people benefit from riding with training wheels, while others (the "naturals") pick up skills as they go and flourish. And while you might never get the chance to take mind-broadening courses such as law and sociology, jurisprudence, and vegetable rights, they might not do you any good if you never learn the skills that enable you to apply that nice, broad brain.

Special Offerings

Most law schools offer the same fundamental courses, especially first year. But there are special programs or special emphases at certain law schools that you should be aware of. The following examples are given solely to alert you to the kinds of things you can find out there and are not meant to disparage similar programs at other schools:

- **Public interest law.** In a few short years of existence, the City University of New York/School of Law at Queens College has emerged as *the* public-interest law school. The proof: More than two-fifths of its graduates go into public-interest law, compared to an average of 2 percent nationwide.

- **Communications law.** Washington D.C.'s Catholic University is a fulcrum in the teaching and academic development of communications law. Not surprising, since the school closely cultivates externships at the federal agencies including those that make communications policy.

- **Environmental law.** A hundred years ago the northwestern corner of the United States was in Chicago; today it's Portland, Oregon, home to Lewis and Clark College's Northwestern School of Law and its nationally-recognized environmental law program. In Westchester County, New York's Pace University watches that beat on the East Coast.

- **Animal rights.** If you think beasties have rights and would be interested in spending some time advocating on their behalf, there's no place like Rutgers University, Newark, New Jersey. That's because only Rutgers has an Animal Rights Clinic.

- **Banking law.** Boston University offers an advanced law degree in banking law, so you might want to go there if you really like money.

- **Computer law.** Many law schools are devoting resources and thought to this burgeoning area, but one of the innovators continues to be the Illinois Institute of Technology/Chicago–Kent College of Law in Chicago.

- **Social policy.** Berkeley/Boalt Hall's program in Jurisprudence and Social Policy draws on that school's renowned social-sciences faculty. It's regarded as a model of interdisciplinary study.

- **Health law.** The University of Houston Law Center is a national leader in the area of law that concerns merely one-seventh of the national economy, and seven sevenths of the national population: Health and medicine.

- **Trial advocacy.** One of the most outstanding and rigorous clinical programs for would-be trial lawyers is in Buies Creek, North Carolina, at Campbell University/Norman Adrian Wiggins School of Law. At Campbell, you *will* learn how to try cases.

- **Natural resources law.** If you had the kind of natural resources they have in and around Boulder, Colorado, you'd fight for them, too. They certainly do at the esteemed Natural Resources litigation clinic at the University of Colorado. For a similar reason, you might want to look at the University of New Mexico.

- **Tax law.** Maybe it's because of all those retirees, or maybe it has something to do with the business Mecca of Disney, but in Florida tax is a big topic. One of the best places to learn about tax law is the University of Florida in Gainesville.

Keep in mind that not every program at every school is open to every student. Often there are a limited number of slots in certain clinics. And remember, only the most securely self-directed types should choose a law school for a single clinical program. You may think you know what you want to specialize in, but life is full of surprises.

QUALITY OF LIFE

Law students tend to get melodramatic about how difficult their lot is, and discussions of quality of life in law school are often full of jokes about which "circle of hell" a particular school is in. The main difference between law school and hell, however, is not the toil, but the exit door. Hell doesn't have one.

But your three years in law school can be more or less pleasant based on subjective quality-of-life issues such as:

- **Neighborhood.** Some of the best schools are in some of the most depressed neighborhoods. Other schools undoubtedly attract people who, other things being equal, would rather be near the beach, the slopes, or the clubs. All that may not matter to you, depending on how much you get out. But if it does matter, don't write it off.

- **Community.** This is the one inside the four walls of law school. Some places are renowned for their uptightness, others for their laid-backness. You may want to avoid the kind of place where people razor pages out of law books so others working on the same assignment can't use them (it really does happen), unless you like that sort of thing. Some people put a lot of stock in how closely faculty and students interact and consider this a big factor in "quality of life." Others aren't really interested in hanging out with people who've made federal jurisdiction their lives.

- **Diversity.** This, too, is a matter of taste. Do you crave a law school class that is a rich broth of different cultures, races, religions, and regional outlooks? Or could you care less? From school to school there are vastly differing attitudes towards diversity, much less executions of it, so get a handle on the respective states of your prospective schools.

- **Extracurricular activities.** Has anyone ever chosen a law school on the basis of extracurricular activities offered there? Probably not. But they can be part of your quality-of-life evaluation, and also act as barometers of other aspects of student life. Is there an active Federalist Society (conservative and libertarian) and no National Lawyers Guild (liberal), or vice-versa? Other typical student organizations include, under various names, black, Jewish, Hispanic, and other minority law student associations, groups for women law students, and other political interest, and sometimes service groups. Some schools also have groups for students interested in going into a particular area of practice.

FACILITIES

It doesn't matter whether a law school has 150,000, 400,000, or one million volumes in its law library. You're not likely to do much legal research while in law school beyond what's found in the state and federal law reporters, the accompanying digests, the standard reference texts, and the law reviews. Every law school has these, though when it comes to law reporter volumes, the number of sets on hand can make a big difference the night before your legal writing assignment is due.

Also, the law library is a place you'll spend a lot of time. You should check it out, and find out from students as much as you can. Is there room to study? Are there lockers for your stuff? Is it well lit? Are there enough computerized research terminals? And—if you didn't learn this in college—for goodness sake, are there enough copiers? (And are they, and their money-vacuuming systems, reliable?)

The Grass Is Always Greener

Having a shiny new library isn't always all it's cracked up to be. Northwestern University built a state-of-the-art law school building in the early 1980s, overlooking Lake Michigan. Its students relished the idea of settling in at their new facility, which replaced an ancient and outmoded building. Unfortunately for the Nor'westerners, so did law students from Northern Illinois University *(located in DeKalb, a suburb of Chicago), as well as from other Chicago schools such as DePaul University, John Marshall Law School, Loyola University—even downtown rival, the University of Chicago. The law library was open to "all members of the Chicago legal community," whether they paid Northwestern's top-of-the-line tuition or not.*

But to rub it in just a little more, Northwestern students would return from dinner to find tables, carrels, and study rooms occupied by . . . Northwestern students. Northwestern medical students.

The economists at the U. of C. would call this a "free-rider" problem. But under the terms of city-wide agreements on mutual access to facilities, much less the needs of medical students whose own library was insufficient, there wasn't much the Northwestern administration could do. It eventually put someone in place to check IDs to ensure that only "legitimate" free riders were hopping on board and that outside law students' access was limited during the weeks before exams. The university also saw to it that the medical schools' facilities would be improved as well.

Beyond the library, some schools are more pleasant and effectual environments for learning than others. It's not a great idea to commit to attending a school sight unseen, especially if you're someone who's distracted by your environment. And, of course, if you have special needs because of a disability, you should find out how well prospective schools can accommodate you.

Where to Live

Not all of your sleeping will be in Trusts and Estates class. So be sure and get the story about dormitories and off-campus housing. Some schools include beautiful photographs of their fine stock of housing, but inform admitted students only later that there's virtually no room at the inn. Others have rooms available, but ones that will make you wish they hadn't. If you want to, or have to, live off campus, get a realistic picture of what and where the options are. Some schools will help match you with a potential roommate; certainly, schools that don't have adequate student housing should do no less for out-of-towners.

Wired

The charm of ivy, brick, and dusty old copies of Black's Law Dictionary aside, law schools now have to keep up with modern technology and maintain adequate computing facilities, meaning:

- An adequate number of relatively up-to-date terminals in the law school building
- The capacity to access the school network from off-campus or, ideally, wired-in dorm rooms
- Free electronic mail and Internet access for students
- A competent and accessible computing support staff
- Computer training

One of the things your generation of law school will bring to its employers is more computing savvy than most senior lawyers have. Your law school should do everything it can to help you take advantage of your technological edge. These skills will be very important after law school in the real world.

CHAPTER TEN

Getting In

Chances are that if you're serious enough about law school to have purchased this book and to have read this far, there's a law school seat out there for you. That seat may not be in the school or even in the city you'd hoped for; it may not be available this fall. On the other hand it may be at the school of your dreams. Either way, you've taken the first step on the road to becoming an attorney.

The Old-Fashioned Way

Thomas M. Cooley Law School in chilly Lansing, Michigan is one of the few law schools left where the clichéd words of the first year of law school ("Look to your left. Look to your right. By the end of this year, one of you will be gone") are even close to true. That's because Cooley does it the old-fashioned way: It admits more students than it intends to graduate, and really weeds them out in the course of the year.

At Cooley—its median admission's GPA 2.46, its median LSAT 148—the idea is to admit almost everyone, with more than four-fifths of applicants invited to enroll. Once that invitation is accepted, Cooley students have to prove their stuff. One test is their ability to put up with a three-year curriculum where 80 percent of courses are mandatory. Fifteen percent of those who start flunk out.

There are 150,000 people who will take the LSAT this year. But don't let that number discourage you; that's the number of people who may have no more than a casual interest in attending law school. Two-thirds of them will go beyond the casual to actually applying to a law school or two, or twelve. Ultimately, there's room for about

40,000 warm bodies to start law school this year. So among those who apply, your chances are a little less than half of getting into some law school.

Still a little discouraged? Don't be. There's much you can do to improve your odds, taking advantage of the strengths you have to offer. Doing those things is the topic of this chapter.

Admissions Competition

As a result of your thoughts on where to go to law school after what you read in the last chapter, you should have a decent and realistic idea of the law schools to which you would want to apply.

Most admissions decisions (especially the "no"s) are made strictly by the numbers. That means most are made fast; as in less time than it took you to read this sentence.

What does "realistic" mean? You have a college education, and you had to go through the applications process to get it. So you don't need charts or graphs to tell you that if you have 2.9 GPA and an LSAT of 160, you're in line for a different set of schools than someone with a 3.8 GPA and the same LSAT. Finding out which is which is beyond the scope of this book; again *The Princeton Review Student Access Guide to the Best Law Schools* is your ticket. But here we can address general rules that are more than generalities.

How true is the phrase "numbers rule"? Law schools do care about subjective criteria. They consider your background, extracurricular activities, academic concentration, where you went to college, and, if you've been out of school for a while, what you've done since college and how well you've done it. But: *Law schools mostly care about these things to distinguish among candidates who already meet their basic standards for consideration*—a blend of GPA and LSAT.

Selling Success

You'll start getting information from law schools almost as soon as you sign up for the LSAT (see below). The LSAT kit also comes with materials that enable you to get applications and other materials from law schools, and you can order many of them online as well. These materials are not bad sources of information, but of course they are marketing materials. Their purpose is promotion. Though you probably won't see outright falsehoods in brochures sent out by law schools, focus on the hard facts they present, not the dreamy photos of ivy-covered gargoyles.

As your focus on where to apply improves, start working on those applications early. Last-minute submissions are bound to be full of mistakes. Though your essay will fundamentally be the same from school to school, you will have to adapt it depending on how a school phrases its personal statement section. It's a good idea to make photocopies of applications so you can fill out a practice version of each one and avoid screwups.

Some law schools work on rolling admissions; they'll accept applications from some point in the fall, through the spring, and admit people as they come. With these schools, it obviously pays to apply early. Other schools won't even let you send an application before, say January; they'll just throw it away. Others will accept them from the fall on, but apprise all applicants of their status on a uniform date, such as April 1. In any case, while you don't want to rush your application, it's good not to push the deadline.

That doesn't mean you're not entitled to apply to one or two long-shot schools if you want to. It just means you should focus your energies and spend your application-fee dollars on the best schools among those that are in your league. Again, if you really want it, you can probably have it; "it" being a law degree and a legal career. That, once again, is the critical determination.

Affirmative Action

Whenever a discussion ensues about admissions "numbers"—GPAs and board scores—the controversial specter of affirmative action looms not far behind. Affirmative action is a policy under which candidates who are members of certain designated groups are given opportunities that, based on objective criteria, they would not otherwise get. Affirmative action is meant to remedy the historical wrong done to a minority group by making available special access and opportunities to them.

Many people believe that affirmative action is a reasonable approach to rectifying generations of injustice that have prevented society's best opportunities from being enjoyed by members of victimized groups. Some say it is not enough, and falls way short of what is needed to remedy past discrimination. Others believe that affirmative action replaces one form of discrimination with another. One thing is for sure: The existence of affirmative action has affected some perceptions of minority group members who are benefited by it, causing them to be viewed by others as recipients of "special treatment."

Thus some African-Americans report that they have to achieve even more to be taken at the same value as others with comparable credentials, because of the presumption that, because they are black, they need not have achieved as much as whites who have the same credentials. In this regard, affirmative action has to some extent backfired, at least in terms of race relations. It has caused resentment by those denied admission to a school or denied a job offer, supposedly in favor of a "less qualified" minority-group member.

But this is more about perception than reality. No one should consider himself a person who would have gotten into a law school "but for" slots filled by candidates whose applications were considered in light of affirmative action policies. Though believing that to be the case may make some people feel better about their disappointment, the truth is that most people who don't make it just don't make it.

The hard facts are that, in order to allow a virtual tripling of African-American representation in law schools between 1972 and 1992, as well as a six-fold increase in Asian Americans, a tripling of Hispanic Americans, and almost two-and-a-half times as many American Indians, non-minority representation among the law school population decreased by only a tenth. That's only a percentage, by the way; considering the growth in the number of law school seats available since 1972, there are more "European Americans" in law school now than there were before widespread affirmative action.

The fact that few individuals can point to affirmative action as a source of their woes is especially true at the most selective schools, where there's no one in the class of any color who isn't extraordinarily well-qualified. That marginal person who was this close to getting in and, but for affirmative action, didn't, is virtually certain to have *gotten in somewhere else appropriate to her level of achievement.*

None of this is to suggest an answer to the hotly debated merits of affirmative action. But whether you think the policy is "justice delayed" or "reverse discrimination," your responsibility to yourself—to put together the best possible credentials, and present them in the best light —is unchanged. Ultimately, everyone reaps what he himself sows.

ACADEMIC PERFORMANCE

In chapter 7 you were urged to major in what you love, and that if you can't find what you love, then at least what you like. As warm and fuzzy as that sounds, it's actually a little cold and calculating. You will do better at what you like; you will get better grades when you do better; you will have more choices about where to attend law school if you have better grades. So you see, love conquers all.

Does that mean that a candidate with an A– average (3.7 GPA) and a major in pasta studies is the equivalent to one with an A– average and a major in molecular biology? In one sense, yes; when the first sweep is made and all candidates with a certain profile and a certain LSAT/GPA combination are eliminated, both will indeed be treated the same.

There is a point where applications are read by human eyes, and when they are, the grownups are separated from the kiddies. Besides the fact that law school admissions officers attended college themselves, they are especially keen students of what majors, and courses, are what. If both candidates make the first cut (or perhaps the first two cuts) based on their numbers, and there was only one seat left in the law school of their mutual dream, you'd want to have your money on the person with the more demanding curriculum. So no, ultimately they're not the same.

But, again, initially they *are* the same. And, sad but true, if the macaroni man (the pasta major, that is) had an *A* average (4.0 GPA), he'd have a leg up on the biologist. More importantly, if that same pasta major had himself majored in biology and only pulled a 3.7, he'd be worse off than in the course he did follow.

Exchange Rates

Now who ever heard of a pasta major? Certainly not anyone who went to a very good college or even a very decent one (unless, of course, it was culinary school). The next point to consider in terms of what you bring to the table in academic credentials is where that GPA was earned.

The Local Currency

If GPAs from different schools are thought of as various currencies whose values have to be squared to make comparison possible, the advantage of the "local currency"—applications from undergraduates of the university that is home to a given law school—is obvious. Not surprisingly, law schools get more applications from undergraduates at colleges affiliated with their law schools than from any other single college. In that respect, therefore, the competition might be a little tougher. On the other hand, the experience on many campuses is that the institutional imperative toward this academic nepotism cannot be ignored.

Thus many law schools give extra consideration to these candidates—which is only appropriate. Why should a student's affection for a university, an affection that burns enough to inspire seven years of devoted study—the better part of a decade—not be requited at least a little bit?

An Okie from Muskogee

The best law schools in the country have students from some of the most remote little colleges in the country, even in the world. They *love* people like that, because it makes them feel very broad-minded. But they don't have *too many* of those types, either. Those who do come from lesser-known programs tend to be outstanding (depending, of course, on the law school). What they mostly have is people who have excelled at the most competitive colleges in the country.

This is true down the line. After all, there is a premise that most grades are achieved on a curve of some sort or another. So the meaning of a GPA is limited to its context. If your undergraduate competition wasn't so competitive, you have to really distinguish yourself to indicate special promise.

You may ask why a consideration such as where a GPA was achieved, essential as it is to evaluating academic achievement, is not included in the first look at your GPA. One answer is that it would be too hard. Another answer is that it's built in, depending on the weight assigned to it by the school. Thus, a law school may well evaluate averages differently, but anyone with a 2.8 GPA probably isn't worth considering regardless of where they went to school. The next cut could involve these finer distinctions.

Exactly how your school is reckoned in a specific admissions office is hard to say. There could be an alumnus of your college on the admissions staff (though that could cut either way), or the admissions officer may never have heard of your college. Admissions offices also know which colleges have the worst "gradeflation," where no one suffers worse than a C without assaulting the professor (Stanford), or where Ds and Fs are simply not reported on a transcript (Brown).

You probably have a good idea of where your college shines in the constellation of higher education, and whether or not there's a "gradeflation" quotient there. Your academic accomplishments ultimately reflect the brightness of your school's light.

The Academic Atlas

An issue related to your undergraduate school's reputation is the law school's desired geographical distribution. This is often a function of what population the law school sees itself as serving. If a law school is local, and satisfied with being a local school, it will have neither a policy nor an interest favoring those from far-flung locales. If it's a state school, it almost certainly has a large percentage of seats set aside for in-state residents, which can be good or bad depending on the state you're in.

On the other end of the scale, national schools do desire some degree of geographic diversity but seldom have to worry much about getting it. Still, an application from Utah—assuming, again, it makes the first cut—may catch a tad more attention at Columbia than an otherwise equivalent one from Long Island.

In fact, the New York area is full of law schools, including quite a few that are among the most highly regarded. It's also full of colleges, which are also many of the most respected institutions (and often the same ones). Ultimately, the darn place is full of people, i.e., competition. This is the least desirable place to live if you want to get into one of these schools, or, for that matter, one in New England or the West Coast, both areas being populated with more than a few easterners.

What this means is that if you're from a densely-populated area, from which there are likely to be many potential applicants, you've got to leave yourself more room for disappointment. This includes not only the New York area but any major city, especially those surrounded by dense suburbs of relatively wealthy expatriate families of that city, e.g., "Chicagoland," greater Washington, and Los Angeles.

Dwellers in these greater metropolises have to apply to more schools to increase their chances. And it wouldn't hurt to look to other regions for opportunity, as well. One approach, though not always available, is to look for a swell in the ocean of schools that you can ride to the top.

For example, consider the case of the New Yorker who isn't exactly a shoe-in at Columbia or NYU. While the University of Chicago and UCLA won't necessarily be looking to round out their classes with easterners—they're just that competitive—there may be schools that are ascending in the rankings or that have their eyes on "national" or enhanced "regional" status. These institutions may be willing to cut a break to someone from an eastern school. Doing so increases their visibility on that campus in the years to come, so they might garner more highly-qualified students. It also gives up-and-coming schools a rationale to attract recruiting interest from the East, since firms are only interested in interviewing students who are likely to want to live (as opposed to spend the summer) where they're located.

And what if you're the Mickey Mantle of prelaw students—a freckle-faced farm kid with great boards and a 3.6 from the University of Oklahoma? If that's the case, good news: If you were never a special person before, you are a special person now.

Take a look at the numbers to see where your chances lie. Some examples of median GPAs at various schools: At Harvard, it's 3.83; at a national school such as Georgetown, it's 3.53. Marquette University in Milwaukee straddles the middle with a median of 3.14. And the mean at newly-accredited New England School of Law in Boston is 2.95.

THE LAW SCHOOL ADMISSIONS TEST

You have to take the LSAT—kind of a grown-up SAT with fangs—to get into law school. This can be good or bad, depending on whether or not you do well on it, and how the respective law schools you apply to count your LSAT score in their admissions formula.

The LSAT Season

The LSAT is given in February, June, October, and December. You may want to prepare for your first one in June of your junior year. Think of it as an "early return" that will enable you to get an idea as to where you stand. But the most common time to take the test is in October of senior year.

Unlike the SAT, it doesn't necessarily pay to take the LSAT more than once. Few people do. Scores don't usually rise significantly in subsequent tests. You should accomplish your practice by practicing, not in real time. Your scores will be averaged in the uniform statistical information provided by the Law School Data Assembly Service (LSDAS)—another LSAC sideline—to all law schools to which you apply. You're allowed to cancel an LSAT if you immediately know something went awfully wrong.

Applications for the LSAT, called the LSAT/LSDAS Registration and Information Book, are available from your prelaw advisor, or by contacting LSAC directly at:

Box 2000
661 Penn Street
Newton PA 18940-0998

(215) 968-1001

Like most academic "boards," the LSAT is mostly a test of your ability to take that particular board. Despite claims to the contrary, its ability to predict how you will do in law school, much less as a lawyer, is quite questionable. (More recent claims that it predicts only first-year success are a little more credible.) The consensus is that the LSAT is as hard as any standardized board test, which, considering how many people think they want to go to law school, is not surprising. Its purpose is weeding out the "unfit," whether they'd be good law students or not.

Perhaps the most damning thing about the LSAT is that it's a multiple-choice test, a fairly rare thing in law school, where you may have to choose the "best answer" among several that are correct, or of which none are correct. Mastering this skill is purportedly analogous to fine analytical ability, but the very exercise itself is so antithetical to the way lawyers approach problems (especially in the Anglo-American common-law system) that the decision to employ it raises questions that are unanswerable in this space.

Nonetheless, you're not going anywhere without it.

The LSAT and Admissions

So how much does the LSAT count? It depends on the philosophy of the law school. Some schools count it less than GPA. Some count it more—as much as two times more. Someone with a great GPA is in good shape with anything short of a disastrous LSAT, but she'd be in better shape with a great LSAT. On the other hand, someone with mediocre grades can vastly improve his admissions credibility by earning LSAT scores that put him in the "big leagues." Suddenly, mediocrity looks like untapped potential. The other possibility—lousy grades, lousy scores—need not be pursued.

Scoring and Structure

So what's a "good score"? That depends on where you want to go to law school. But here are the basics:

The LSAT is scored on a scale of 120 to 180. The average is 150. Along with your score you get a percentile rank, which indicates the percentage of people who took the test who have scored lower than you in the last five years. You want this number to be as close to 99 as possible, but remember that your LSAT peers are motivated, brighter than average, and have honed their test-taking skills.

There are about a hundred scored questions on the test, which is broken into five sections:

- Two are "arguments" sections, where you read and analyze a passage in which the author puts forth some conclusion based on certain premises and assumptions.

- One is a reading comprehension section; these first three sections will remind you of the verbal SAT.

- The fourth section is called "Games," though there's nothing fun about it. The "games" are puzzles that supposedly test your ability to make conceptual deductions, typically, more the work of detectives than lawyers.

- There's a fifth section called "experimental," which can be a recapitulation of any of the previous types of section. It's used to help the LSAT people develop future LSAT tests. You don't have to volunteer for this "experiment"; your contribution to next year's torment is mandatory. (Though you might guess which section is the experimental one, you never really know.)

- There's also an essay section. It was added to the LSAT when someone felt guilty that writing ability—maybe the single most important skill you can and should measure in a prospective law student—wasn't measured. It's still not measured. The essays aren't graded; law schools have the "option" of reading them. You can guess how much time they'll spend on that, but of course you don't dare do less than your best on this.

The score of 180 is deemed statistically "perfect," even though you could miss a few questions and still achieve it. One reason for that is some versions of the LSAT are harder than others, and the test people (the Law School Admissions Council) know it.

To give you a sense of what different scores will get you: The median LSAT score at Yale, the most selective law school in the Milky Way, is 171, or around the ninety-eighth percentile. At a highly-respected state school such as the University of Indiana, it's 161 (eighty-sixth percentile). And at a newish school in a region full of law schools, Touro College – Jacob D. Fuchsberg Law Center in Huntington, New York, the median LSAT is 151, just a squidge above the halfway mark in scoring and percentile.

Plugola

If you hadn't heard, The Princeton Review does a little bit of test-preparation when it isn't publishing books such as this. The Princeton Review's "take" on the LSAT is not the same as those of other test-prep courses. The best

place to read about the LSAT is in the latest edition of
The Princeton Review's Cracking the LSAT, though The
Student Advantage Guide to Law School also has more
detailed information.

But regardless of which course you take or which book
you buy, the only way to prepare for the LSAT is practice,
practice, practice—especially with timed simulations of
the test and especially with real LSATs. You can get
these through the LSAC. It would not be overkill to spend
eighty hours preparing for the LSAT. It's only the gate-
way to your career, after all.

SUBJECTIVE FACTORS

Now you understand that grades and LSATs are the alpha and omega
of law school admissions. But even if your numbers get you into the
running, unless you're a Phi Beta Kappa (or darn close), you have to
distinguish yourself from the pack if you want to have a choice in
where you attend law school. Even if you are a Phi Beta Kappa, there
isn't enough room in the best law schools for all of you. There are a
number of other factors that, past the quantitative winnowing, go into
the admissions decision:

- Recommendations
- Personal statement/essay
- Work experience
- Extracurricular activities
- Community involvement

Be aware that law school applications don't necessarily highlight
the importance of questions that elicit this information. After identifying which of the above (it could be all) you want to get across,
look for the spot on the application that gives you an opening, and—
within reason—run with it.

Recommended Reading

Law schools require two, or sometimes three, letters of recommendation. Each application comes with a form that you submit to the
recommender for this purpose, but most recommenders write a single

letter that stays on file in the prelaw office (or however your school works it) and just gets stapled to that form.

Who should write your letter of recommendation? The law school applications are shooting straight when they tell you:

- It should be someone who knows you well enough to meaningfully comment on your abilities. "Well enough" ideally means knows you by your name.

- As if this weren't obvious from the preceding, don't bother with a letter from a prominent alumnus of the school, public official, or "bar leader" who doesn't know you. None of these people are in any real position to exercise power to get you admitted, and if they don't know you well enough to write that really meaningful evaluation, it's a big waste at best. At worst, it makes you look insincere, shallow, and manipulative.

What the law schools won't tell you is the most obvious point of all: Choose someone who's familiar with work you've done *well*. Ideally this will be someone who can point to a specific achievement or project that he is familiar with, and who won't mind writing about it in the recommendation. Don't be shy about reminding the professor of that groundbreaking paper you completed in his class.

Some conscientious recommenders want to know more about you than they might have gleaned from their limited exposure to you in class. Have a resume or, better yet, a more detailed and personal *curriculum vitae* prepared for that purpose. It's worth letting the recommender know that, say, you're the first person in your family ever to have gone to college, that you paid for college by selling your blood plasma, or other such stuff that might be too maudlin for the personal essay (see below).

As for the role of the application essay, some advise that you provide this to the recommender as well. The idea behind this is to present a theme or at least a consistent message in the application package.

Professional Recommendations

People who've been out of college for any substantial amount of time are expected to come up with letters of recommendation from people for whom they have worked. All the factors outlined above for getting recommendations from professors apply here too. You want someone who really knows you and your work; you want specifics; and you want the message to be about your potential and, especially in professional recommendations, your ability to demonstrate commitment.

But, if it's not too late, get a professor or former professor to write one for you too. If you don't need it now, ask them to keep it on file. Ideally, you *should* have an academic one in your application. Only former teachers can speak directly to your scholastic talent. Without this, only your grades (and, ostensibly, your LSATs) will have anything to say about the one subject law schools care about most.

One last point: You'll probably never meet anyone in law school or the legal profession who can point to a letter of recommendation that made the difference in getting into law school. That in itself isn't too compelling, since most people don't find out what got them in. But an *ex post facto* evaluation of where you get in is likely to suggest that all the factors you expect to be there—grades, scores, etc.—*are* there. Will a recommendation separate you from similarly-situated applicants? You'll probably never know.

So the recommendation is a bit of a black box, especially since it will never be read by you. (Some law schools allow you to submit nonconfidential recommendations and to indicate if you have done so on the recommender form. *Forget it.*) Only the most extraordinary recommendation is likely to make the difference for you. But, like so much else in this process, you've got to do your best to put together the best stuff you can.

The Essay

The application essay, or personal statement, is the only wholly subjective (from your point of view) component of the law school application. Regardless of how a given law school chooses to phrase its "question," you are essentially going to explain who you are and why you want to go to law school.

Think of this exercise as your first assignment in legal writing. You have to convince the court (the admissions office) that you are special, and that you've thought about why you want to go to law school. Now that you've read through this book, there's every reason to believe you know what to say by the time you're writing essays.

But, as in all good advocacy, you have to make your case without insulting the reader's intelligence, stretching your credibility, or (the worst crime of all) boring him. Remember, brevity is the soul of wit. That admissions officer has a lot of reading to do. He's not going to do a lot of reading on *your* essay unless you're Hemingway. Chances are, you're not.

And speaking of Hemingway, you have to demonstrate your overall competence to make your argument. That means the craftsmanship on the personal statement must be the best you can produce. In the case of a legal brief, a spelling error brings into doubt your carefulness in conducting your legal research. Here that effect is amplified (and it may also suggest that you can't spell).

Here are some basic tips to keep in mind while working on that personal statement:

- **Size matters.** Maximum length of the essay should be two, *maybe* three, typed double-spaced pages.

- **Testing 1-2-3.** Don't rationalize a less-than-brilliant LSAT score by kvetching how you're "not a good test taker." Taking tests is what you do in law school. And it sounds like baloney anyway.

- **Accentuate the positive.** Rather than focus on this "test taking" problem, slam home how good you are at . . . well, whatever it is you're good at, and make it something that law schools like. Not skateboarding.

- **Grading your grades.** If your grades, rather than your LSATs, are the problem, there is some wiggle room to address this topic. The key is to offer an alternative criterion by which to judge your smarts and, no less important, your ability to apply them. (If your cumulative GPA was dragged down by an anomalous semester or a course grade, this might be worth addressing.) Keep in mind here that you have to get across why you're ready to apply strengths previously reserved for extra-curricular activities, work, or God to your new passions in life: Contracts, Torts, and Civil Procedure.

- **A divine calling.** Speaking of which, don't bother impressing the committee with your lifelong desire to become a member of the noble bar-blah-blah. Besides sounding like you're begging, this information is not much more meaningful vis-à-vis the admissions decision than if you told them you always wanted to be a fireman or a ballerina. Mature reflection is what's called for here, not pat autobiography.

- **Justice, justice pursuest thou.** Don't claim you want to go to law school to right society's wrongs unless you're damn sure you mean it and are prepared to say what you have in mind and why. Remember that most people go to law school to increase their earning potential. They know this.

- **Did I mention my fine grades?** The only reason anyone's reading your personal statement is because your GPA and LSAT didn't eliminate you. If you've got something to crow about, don't crow about it here. The exception is if the GPA tells a tale. If you achieved a 3.4 GPA by the fall of junior year after having flatlined at 2.0 all of freshman year, now *that's* "man bites dog"—a newsworthy story.

Remember to check and recheck your work, and have someone else look at it too. Accept the critiques like a grownup. If you're not prepared to put in that much effort on this critical project, you aren't going to last very long as a lawyer anyway.

Work Experience

Law school applications often ask for information about work, such as whether you worked while in college, and, if so, how much. Obviously this works to the advantage of those who have worked, especially if they could use a little help on the GPA front. Law schools generally will factor a meaningful amount of time spent earning your education into consideration of your GPA. It also suggests a bit of character and maturity to see that someone's done something besides live off her parents' money.

The second bit of work-related information is the line in the application that asks for a description of "significant professional accomplishments." This is meant for people who have worked full-time after college, although if you achieved a significant professional accomplishment in a campus or school-year job, you might want to finesse that in here. (Just watch the overkill; don't mention it both here and in your essay.)

If you have a resume that reflects your post-college accomplishments, and the application gives you room to submit it, do so. Just be sure to also submit it to the same checking and review process as you do any other application material.

Your answer to this question on the application should, however, be a tad more moderate than typical resume puffing. Keep exaggeration to a minimum. If you have something to say about your employment-related accomplishments in terms of how they have directed your focus toward a legal career or have given you the opportunity to demonstrate assiduousness and responsibility, let that be incorporated into your personal statement.

Extracurricular Activities

Extracurricular activities have been addressed already, in chapter 7. A quick review: The main thing extracurricular activities do in terms of getting into law school is lower your GPA. That isn't a help. If you are single-mindedly determined to get into the absolutely, positively best law school you can, you will drop all thoughts of taking the one chance in your life for a rich and well-rounded college experience and stay in the library from September through May.

Yes, law schools prefer a well-rounded 3.7 to a square 3.7, but they prefer a 3.7 to a 3.4. And how about a 3.31 "with" the debate team versus 3.37 "without" it? Let's not ask silly questions. You can't predict how extracurricular activities are going to affect your GPA with any degree of precision. It comes down, once again, to whether you're going to be "a prelaw" or a human being who's attending college and considering a legal career down the road. The former will eschew the once-in-a-lifetime opportunities that the real world probably won't afford her—whether it's saber-fencing, rowing crew, high-kicking in a musical revue, or broadcasting at 10,000 watts. The latter will make a reasonable attempt to balance academics and a moderate extracurricular load, keeping in mind the preservation of her main purpose for attending college: getting an education.

But here you are, today, filling out the application. Do you mention your extracurricular activities? Of course. And if your grades are a tad lower than they might be (whose aren't?), it's certainly wise not to leave the admissions office with the impression that you spent the last four years in a mosh pit or in a drunken stupor.

The best use of extracurricular activities is when they indicate leadership and sustained commitment to an activity or even a couple of activities. That's a sign of focus and maturity. You may even be able to get across the message (with the help of your personal statement) that you consciously sacrificed a certain degree of academic diligence *at a certain point* because of your commitment to others or to a meaningful undertaking in an extracurricular setting. This won't play for all four years, but it could be a good way to deal with *"that* semester."

Conversely, don't load this part of your application with cow pies. Unless you can use activities to show something substantial of the type discussed above, don't bother with a simple recitation of resume-ballast such as "yearbook staff," "fraternity social committee," or even "prelaw club." Even if these were legitimate activities, they must carry weight on the application, or they'll weigh it down and detract from your message. And if they *are* only ersatz activities, this will be transparent. All it takes is a little incredibility to undermine the whole story, no matter how true the rest of it may be.

Community Involvement

This is about action, not talk. If you have devoted a substantial amount of time to volunteer work, political involvement, or other endeavors that extend around the zone of self-absorption, put it on the application. It helps; again, it demonstrates maturity and something other than the rank careerism that characterizes most professional school applicants. If your personal statement alludes to an interest in public interest law, it is this demonstration of your commitment to the common weal that will make such a claim credible.

If you haven't already rolled up your sleeves and taken the time to involve yourself in helping others, don't rationalize, either to yourself or in the essay, that your busy undergraduate schedule has prevented you from making the commitment you're certain to make as a lawyer. You'll never have more choice about what to do with your time than you do while in college. Law school application time is when you focus on what you have done, not what you would have done.

Afterword

It isn't really all that bad.

At the outset of my thinking about this book, I submitted outlines to The Princeton Review with chapter titles such as "The Art School is Down the Street," "Loudmouths, Paper-Pushers, and Digitheads," and "After All, You'll Always Have the Debt." My attitude at the time was a result of the nearly universal response of my colleagues in the legal profession when they would hear I was writing a book for prelaw students: "Tell them not to go to law school."

But it isn't really that bad. You can have a happy, satisfying, and successful career in law, or even out of law, with a law degree. Thousands of lawyers do. The fact that other thousands love to complain about their work demonstrates little. Many of them are pampered whiners who would complain almost regardless of how things were going. And of course lawyers are verbal people with a penchant for pleading cases. Things aren't annoyances or disappointments; they're tragedies and injustices. Law students pick up on this early.

There's also the possibility that, as people with more talent than average, lawyers' expectations of what their legal careers would be like were unrealistic. To some extent, this is a function of how the profession has changed in the last generation. For many, the brass ring just keeps pulling away farther and farther.

But much of how it turns out is in your hands. The trick is to never let yourself become a zombie—not as "a prelaw," not as a law student, not as a young attorney, or even as an old attorney. The thrust of this book is not to deter you but to challenge you.

I have tried at once to present reality and to get you into the habit of analyzing not only cases and deals but your own career path, the legal and other institutions along that path, and your own motivations and wishes as you follow any of the branches of that path.

In short, I've tried to write the book that I wish I'd read before I started law school. I wouldn't say that if I knew then what I know now, I wouldn't have gone to law school. But many of my choices would have been very different, starting from college and up through my first job. My hope is that with the previous couple of hundred pages under your belt, you'll avoid some pitfalls, minimize some regrets, and take satisfaction in your well thought out plan to pursue a legal education.

The Best Law Schools

The following are the 35 law schools at which students are most satisfied, according to a *National Jurist* ranking based on information obtained from Princeton Review surveys. The *National Jurist* compiled law students' responses to questions on faculty, facilities, and the quality of life on campus.

1996 Rank		Faculty Total	Facilities Total	Quality of Life	Overall Total	1994 Total
1	Washington and Lee	26.92	26.50	27.22	80.64	1
2	Washburn	28.31	26.85	24.23	79.39	5
3	Western New England	27.32	25.11	25.09	77.51	17
4	William and Mary	27.61	21.90	27.30	76.80	81
5	USC	25.80	26.77	23.46	76.03	6
6	Seton Hall	25.49	26.64	22.15	74.27	2
7	U. of Notre Dame	25.07	25.01	24.19	74.27	3
8	Northeastern	25.78	21.94	25.92	73.64	24
9	U. of Virginia	25.91	21.86	25.26	73.02	37
10	Georgetown	25.33	26.33	20.87	72.53	58
11	Brigham Young	24.91	25.76	21.85	72.52	12
12	U. of Cincinnati	25.23	25.05	22.03	72.30	15
13	Vanderbilt	26.72	19.96	24.99	71.67	33
14	U. of Richmond	24.68	25.46	21.35	71.49	20
15	South Texas	25.30	23.22	22.62	71.14	9
16	Yale	25.09	22.33	23.36	70.77	11
17	U. of Washington	24.40	23.99	22.37	70.76	10
18	Arkansas/Little Rock	23.83	25.51	21.41	70.74	13
19	U. of Montana	25.40	21.17	24.06	70.62	16
20	Missouri/Columbia	24.32	24.29	21.85	70.45	23
21	Chicago-Kent	23.71	26.34	20.09	70.14	45
22	U. of Wyoming	24.62	22.29	23.22	70.12	14
23	U. of Utah	25.12	22.15	22.48	69.74	26
24	Wake Forest	24.42	25.31	19.95	69.67	21
25	Nova Southeastern	24.24	24.29	21.08	69.60	65
25	UC-Davis	24.76	20.64	24.21	69.60	18
27	U. Of Maine	25.21	19.13	25.17	69.51	51
28	Widener	24.79	23.59	20.99	69.37	19
29	Willamette	23.18	25.52	20.45	69.14	22
30	Stanford	24.61	23.66	20.84	69.11	48
30	Northwestern	23.42	24.14	21.56	69.11	28
32	U. Of Iowa	23.69	26.10	19.26	69.05	25
33	Cornell	24.21	25.86	18.91	68.98	27
34	New York University	23.51	23.88	21.59	68.97	39
35	Texas Tech	23.89	24.68	20.35	68.92	34

Methodology

The *National Jurist* ranking is based on raw data collected in a Princeton Review-sponsored surveyed of more than 28,000 students at 170 ABA-accredited law schools nationwide conducted during the past two years.

The ranking for overall student satisfication is based on student responses to eleven survey questions in three categories—faculty, school facilities, and quality of life. The ranking used a scoring system based on a 100-point scale.

The Princeton Review scored each question on a 4-point scale. The *National Jurist* assigned each question a weight from 1 to 3.5, based on interviews with students and recent graduates. Each question's raw score was multiplied by the assigned weight to acheive a total score for each category. The total scores for each category were added to acheive a law school's overall score. Numbers were rounded once the overall score was calculated. Schools that tied are assigned the same ranking number.

The faculty category—which was worth 36 percent of the overall score—polled student opinions on quality of teaching (3.5 weight), level of faculty-student relations (2.5 weight), diversity of faculty (1.5 weight), and whether students' work is intellectually challenging (1.5 weight).

The facilities category—which was worth 30 percent of the overall score—measured student assessments of research resources (3.5 weight), library staff (1.0 weight), and facilities generally (3.0 weight).

The quality of life category—which was worth 34 percent of the overall score—measured assessments of the degree of competitiveness amoung students (2.0 weight) and the existence of a strong sense of community (3.5 weight), as well as equal treatment by their peers and faculty (1.5 weight each).

The Princeton Review offers LSAT preparation courses and a multistate bar exam course and publishes an annual book called *The Guide to Law Schools.*

About the Author

Ron Coleman is a commercial litigator in a major New Jersey law firm. He is a graduate of Princeton University and Northwestern University School of Law, and has attended rabbinical academies in New York and Israel. He has been a contributing editor of the American Bar Association's *Student Lawyer* magazine, where his work has garnered him various journalism awards and nominations; a contributor to the *American Bar Association Journal*; and is the author of the *ABA Guide to Consumer Law* (Times Books). Coleman has taught law as an adjunct professor at Seton Hall University School of Law and is a lecturer for Aish HaTorah College of Jewish Studies. He lives in northern New Jersey with his wife, attorney and writer Jane Coleman, and children.